THE SLIGO-LEITRIM WORLD OF
KATE CULLEN 1832-1913

Catherine Theresa Mitchell. Private collection, Dublin.

The
Sligo-Leitrim World
of
Kate Cullen

1832-1913

A 19th Century Memoir Revealed
by
HILARY PYLE

The Woodfield Press

This book was typeset in Ireland by
Gough Typesetting Services for
THE WOODFIELD PRESS
29 Oaklands Terrace, Terenure,
Dublin 6, Ireland.

A catalogue record for this title
is available from the British Library.

ISBN 0-9528453-2-6

This book has been published with the assistance of
Sligo County Council.

Printed in Ireland
by Genprint Ltd.

Contents

List of Illustrations

Foreword

The biography of any remarkable person must begin with the parents. In the case of the Irish poet Susan L. Mitchell, contemporary of Yeats and Synge, her origins in a landowning family from County Leitrim in Ireland were of such interest to her that she urged her mother as an old lady to write her memoirs.

The memoirs, spirited, sometimes convoluted, were never published, but when viewed as a background to one of the prominent personalities of the Anglo-Irish Cultural Renaissance, they go a long way in explaining the ethos out of which Yeats, Lady Gregory, Moore and Synge emerged, and other writers who shaped the character and future of modern Irish literature. They are presented here in an edited narrative, interpolating extracts from letters, with other necessary matter, to fill gaps in what is a frank and lively description of county life in the midlands of Ireland long ago.

Kate Cullen's memoir first came to my attention when I began to be interested in Susan Mitchell, and a cousin handed me a brown, broken-flapped cardboard box stuffed with letters and mementoes reaching back over 150 years. Into a smaller box designed for toothpaste tubes in dozens were wedged cracked picture frames and yellowing photographs, and an exercise book with a shiny black cover filled with writing, supplemented by further written sheets pinned in here and there. Written inside the front cover were the words, 'Reminiscences of My Life. Kate Theresa Mitchell. November 12th 1899. 31 The Mall Sligo', the hand recognisable as that of Susan Mitchell. In amongst the strong flowing letters was interpolated in pencil (in what I later discovered was Kate's handwriting), 'My Candid Opinion of My Relatives'.

With the exercise book came a typescript, 83 pages in length, which is a roughly edited version of what is in the exercise book, and was probably typed by Susan in the *Irish Homestead* office in Dublin where she worked as sub-editor with AE (George Russell). There are other copies of this typescript among the Mitchell family. A smaller typescript of some 30 pages gives further information about the members of the Cullen family. There is no manuscript version of this typescript, which was composed at a later date than the first part of the memoir. It seems that Susan, perhaps contemplating publishing Kate's reminiscences, found them confused, and asked her mother to tell more about the individuals involved.

The typescript, despite a certain amount of editing, has no coherent or chronological narrative, but moves about among memories. However, with the help of the letters that have been preserved, and by reordering the material, it has been possible to reconstruct Kate's life from her earliest years in Skreeney on the Sligo-Leitrim border, through her youth in various rented houses in Dublin, Carrick-on-Shannon and Portlaoise, back to the West, where she was married for 12 years in Carrick-on-Shannon and then settled at the age of forty in Sligo. Originally enjoying the privileged life of the landed gentry, her varying fortunes and her large spread-out family led her to many different experiences, that of mistress of a bank house, then reduced to taking in lodgers, then manageress of a fashionable men's club. She was deeply religious, drawn to the non-conformists as many Protestants of her time were, even though she had been born into the Established Church, and still attended the Church of Ireland when she wished.

Kate Cullen had a lively interest in people of whatever social level, and shows a surprising lack of prejudice according to what one might expect looking back from 150 years later. This would seem to be a result of her upbringing, where, while trained to observe certain rules of behaviour and social modes, she had the freedom to meet all kinds of people. The opening paragraph of her memoir gives a taste of the breadth of her early life. She starts,

> Of my early life I have the most pleasing recollections. It was passed between Skreeney and Shannon Lodge [also in Leitrim]. During a visit of my mother to Clare. . . . I was left with my eldest sister Mary Labatt, at Mount Charles, Co. Donegal, where her husband was a Clergyman. I was there let run about the place with the country children and came home to Skreeney rather wild and unmanageable. I was then left for some time with my father at Skreeney, which I enjoyed more than anything.

And so the memoir continues, passing from recollection to recollection.

Just handling the contents of the cardboard boxes was enough to whet the imagination. The neat ivory-coloured or bland blue envelopes were traced with faded seaweed coloured inks, in loops and strokes made by different hands at different times. Pale, alert, self-conscious faces smiled out of a past that is now forgotten. One treasured memento was a tiny tortoiseshell ball-book, with hurried scribbles of the names of momentary dancing partners – their sweaty necks and warm nervous arms around the waist unmentioned. The whole carried the sense of a life left merely behind a corner, through which was revealed an urgent image of the hybrid 'Ascendancy' of Ireland's vanished history.

Kate it is true concentrates on the 'pleasing recollections'. She says little about the Famine, though she assisted her eldest sister Mary Labatt with her ministrations when it was at its height. She hardly refers to political happenings, even though she watched Parnell's public appearances with her excited daughters, and from the letters it is obvious that the family had a social conscience and were interested in public affairs.

Her memoir however is very personal, and has an essential place in local history as the surviving annals of an important county family with all its fortunes and misfortunes.

Among the many people who have assisted me in editing this document I would like to mention especially George Mitchell who gave me the memoir with the family papers and letters from which I have worked, and which have now been presented to the Library, Trinity College, Dublin.

Other members of the family, Kitsy Mitchell, Michael McGuinness and the late Michael Herman Franklin, Kate's great nephew, have been most helpful, as were the late Fitzroy Pyle, and the late Dr Elizabeth Fitzpatrick, who first read my manuscript and made pertinent comments.

Lavinia McCarthy, Fergus Pyle, Peter Ringwood, the Witt Library of the Courtauld Institute, the National Gallery of Ireland and the Representative Church Body helped with the illustrative material.

For information about specific places I have gone to Shane Flynn of Carrick-on-Shannon, Eddie Fraser of Sligo, the Knight of Glin, Pádraig O Snodaigh, and Maevan Healy-Singh, as well as the various libraries in Dublin, Cork and Sligo, including the Representative Church Body Library, Dublin. Dean Browne, Canon D.L. Keegan, Canon Bertie Neill and the Reverend Philip Knowles assisted in tracing the births, marriages and deaths of the Cullen family.

I have been very much buoyed by the enthusiasm of Helen Hartnett, with her helpful editorial comments, and by Terri McDonnell, publisher, with whom it has been a pleasure to work. Also thanks to Lorcan Donnellan whose sensitive approach to the cover design is very much appreciated.

Finally my thanks to the board and staff of the Tyrone Guthrie Centre, Annaghmakerrig, for a haven in which to start writing, and to my family, especially Sorcha and Dúinseach for undertaking the arduous task of indexing, and my husband Maurice, for such interest and support.

* * * * * *

The chapter titles have all been taken from the poems of Susan L. Mitchell, the sources listed at the end of the book.

PATRICK CULLEN = ISABELLA Nesbit
of Skreeney, Manorhamilton dau. of Carn Cross Nesbit
d.1774 of Aughamore, Co. Roscommon

PATRICK = Judith Wynne
d.1775 dau. of Owen
Wynne of Hazelwood
Rector of
Manorhamilton

CARN CROSS = Elizabeth Soden
of Skreeney, dau. of James Soden
Rector of
Manorhamilton

Judith Anne

4 other sons
+ daughters

Carn Cross = Hester JOHN JAMES = BRIDGET
of Skreeney Dickson of Skreeney Finucane
d.1801

Henry Francis Catherine Jane Eliza
Palmer Gledstanes (1) Jones
(2) Campbell

CARN CROSS = Jane Palmer
of Glenade dau. of Catherine
d.1878 Palmer (née Cullen)

Carn Cross 6 daughters
d.1878

Carn Cross Mary Bessie Giles John Marcus Diana Patrick Georgina James Jane Francis KATE = Michael
m. m. [Paddy] m. [Jemmy] m. Nesbit (Catherine Thomas Mitchell
Rev. Noblett (1) Faris Jack Elliot Rev. Noble b.1830 Theresa) 1823-1873
E. Labatt St Leger (2) de l'Herrault Shepperd 1832-1913

George John [Johnny] Bidz Michael [Gilly] SUSAN Jane [Jinny] Victoria [Baby]
Cullen James Finucane Thomas LANGSTAFF Georgina Diana
b.1861 b.1862 b.1863 b.1865 b.1866 b.1868 b.1870

FAMILY TREE OF KATE CULLEN

Meet the Unbroken Family

Skreeney before 1832

Catherine Theresa Cullen, mother of the poet, Susan L. Mitchell – Kate as she was known – came from a typical Anglo-Irish background of the early nineteenth century. She was the youngest of a large family of brothers and sisters, living at Manorhamilton in the County of Leitrim. Their house, Skreeney, 11 Irish miles from Sligo town, had been the residence of the family since the time of Charles I, when Patrick Cullen had come from Scotland to fight with Sir Frederick Hamilton during the rising of 1641.

After the crushing of the Irish, Patrick Cullen established himself not far from Sir Frederick Hamilton's castle, famous for many infamous horrors. In her memoirs, Kate describes Sir Frederick as a man of violent temper, who had no scruples about shedding blood. W.B. Yeats has made his ferocious inhumanity even more vivid in his telling of the murders in Sligo Abbey.[1] It was said that Sir Frederick's brother had been put to death by the Roman Catholics, and that he had vowed to avenge his death by exterminating all of that faith, and making Manorhamilton totally Protestant.

'In consequence of this the story is told that no Catholic who entered the Castle ever left it alive', remarks Kate, and she refers to an incident she heard related by a Mrs Davys of Sligo, who was a descendant of one of Sir Frederick's men, a Mr Rutherford.

> One day, a messenger arriving there, and the usual bloody plan being about to be carried out, one of Sir Frederick's gentlemen, named Rutherford, took pity on the man and contrived his escape. At dinnertime Sir Frederick, on making enquiry about the messenger, discovered that he had escaped.
>
> 'Who let him go?' asked Sir Frederick. 'I did', said Rutherford, without hesitation. 'Very well', said Sir Frederick, 'the gallows that was erected for him will do very well for you and you can take his place at the appointed time.'
>
> So Rutherford sat down and ate his dinner like a man, and at the end of

---

1. *Mythologies*, 1971, pp. 177, etc.

the meal all the gentlemen at table sprang to their feet and swore that, if a finger was laid on Rutherford, there would be a mutiny in the Castle, and Sir Frederick himself would pay the penalty. So Rutherford went scatheless, and it is still said in Manorhamilton that, if you call a little dog 'Rutherford', it will cock its tail!'[2]

The castle was burned to the ground in 1652. The stone gateway to the mile-long drive of Skreeney house still stands beside the ivy smothered ruins of solid towers and Elizabethan windows, which looked much the same during the 1830s of Kate Cullen's childhood as they look today.

Kate's father planted the avenue with a beech hedge, and with sycamore and horse chestnut trees. There was also a fine thorn tree, whose flowing branches reminded Kate of long white feathers. In the driveway near the castle, the family could hear a hollow sound, and they were certain that there were the remains of a secret passageway between the castle and Skreeney house, used during disturbed times as a way of escape. The only attempt to penetrate the passage had been foiled, as foul air had extinguished the candle.

Kate's great-grandfather, another Patrick, was High Sheriff of Manor-hamilton – the town which Sir Frederick had founded and named after himself – in 1782. This Patrick's wife, Isabella Nesbitt of Aughamore, Co. Roscommon, brought the red hair Kate's daughter Susan inherited, and her father's name, Carn Cross,[3] into the family. She was remembered for her bravery. 'The times were rather disturbed when she was living in Skreeney', says Kate.

> My great-grandfather was from home on one occasion and the house was attacked by 'Whiteboys'. My great-grandmother, having armed herself with a 'blunderbuss', shot one of them, and, as the wounded man was trying to get out of the window, she dipped her hand in his blood, and placed it on his back.
>
> It is said that he was afterwards taken by the impress of her hand on his white jacket. This took place in the little room off her bedroom which was afterwards our nursery. She was, I believe, an ugly little red-haired woman, but of indomitable courage.

Patrick and Isabella had six sons, as well as two or three daughters. Patrick was the eldest. His marriage with Judith Wynne, daughter of Owen Wynne, of Hazelwood, Co. Sligo – another descendant of a Cromwellian settler – was

---

2.   Quotations are taken from the typescript of Kate Cullen's memoir.
3.   This is also spelt Carncross in the memoir and letters, with another variant, 'Cairn Cross'. used on the tombstone of Carn Cross Cullen at Youghal.

a connection the family valued. But he had only one child, Judith Anne, who was delicate, and spent most of her life in Florence, and died at Siena, so Kate's grandfather, Carn Cross, succeeded his brother at Skreeney.[4]

Following the practice of the time, Carn Cross, the second son of Patrick and Isabella, had entered the Church. Kate heard that he had been at school at Castleknock in Dublin.[5] Carn Cross entered Trinity College when he was 16, and was ordained in 1775 for a curacy at Ballintemple, near Cavan. At 30, he married Elizabeth, or Ellen, one of the Sodens of Grange in Sligo, who had distinguished themselves as Provosts of the town. Ellen was an heiress of remarkable beauty. A Sligo doctor told Kate Cullen that her grandparents were the handsomest couple who used to ride into Sligo.

After a brief period as a country rector, the Reverend Carn Cross Cullen was appointed to the living of Cloonclare – the ecclesiastical name for Manorhamilton parish – and he could live at home in Skreeney. Manorhamilton Church was handsome – barely 10 years built – and, with an expanding population in mind, was capable of seating 350 worshippers. Inside it spreads an impression of space and light. Outside, the plain stone spire, rising from a spiked and castellated tower, commands the hill above Manorhamilton, the church protected by the surrounding walls of a former military barracks. Graves of parishioners were gradually added in the yard around the church, and in the outlook posts at the four corners of the original barracks, under huge beech trees, the more prominent families were laid to await the last trump. In one of these pleasantly secluded grassy squares, withdrawn in shade from the more companionable centre of the churchyard, Kate's youngest brother Francis lies buried.

Carn Cross Cullen was chaplain to the 10th regiment of militia, the

---

4. Patrick died in 1775. Years later, Susan Mitchell, when she was becoming interested in her antecedents, and her mother's memoirs, copied out the testimony of Judith Anne's friends in the English colony, who recorded on her tombstone at Leghorn that:
   She was no less remarkable for the brilliant faculties of her mind than for the amiable qualities of her heart.
   Candour sincerity and benevolence marked all she said. Sweetness of manner kindness and disinterestedness shewed in everything she did.
   For a bosom friend she would have risked her life, for the afflicted in body or mind the tear of pity dropt, and for the wretched poor her purse was always open.
   This was a cousin worth preserving in the family annals and Susan must have enjoyed the balanced flow of the tombstone's rhetoric.

5. Under Dr Burrowes, immortalised in 19th century Ireland as the author of 'The night before Larry was stretched', an execution ballad, explicit in realistic detail, which has also been attributed to William Maher. According to the Clergy Succession lists in the Representative Church Body Library in Dublin he was also educated by Mr F.D. Kenny, FTCD, before he entered TCD in 1770. He gained a BA in 1774, was ordained for the curacy of Ballintemple (Kilmore Diocese) in 1775, was Vicar of Killan from 1791–2, and from 1792, until his death in 1807, was Rector of Cloonclare.

Leitrim Militia, from 1794 onwards. Two of his brothers, as well as three of his own sons, served in the same regiment, but he himself merely drew a stipend of £7. 15. 0 per month and delegated his duties – the regiment was then stationed at Clonmel – to a deputy.

Life was not always peaceful at Manorhamilton. Kate mentions a traumatic experience during 1798, when her grandfather encountered rebels on the back avenue of Skreeney.

> They passed by almost touching him as he sat on his steady old black horse among the dark trees of the wood: he then escaped to Auburn Grange, near Sligo, the residence of my (Grand) Aunt Manley, his wife's sister, his wife, children and featherbeds having been sent on before him packed in a cart on the news of the coming of the 'Rebels'.

> These were perilous times, and it was well to have a place of refuge. I have been told that the china and all the valuables had been packed into a china closet upstairs by my Grandmother, who got the door papered over, making it look like part of the wall; and the 'Rebels' marched round and round the house seeing a window, but finding no room inside to correspond. So the treasures escaped.

Carn Cross and Ellen had three sons who all chose the army as a career, and became officers in the Leitrim Militia. The heir, Carn Cross, was unfortunate, and never rose above the rank of captain. When he was 18, he was forced to marry Hester Dickson, daughter of Major Dickson of Woodville, Co. Leitrim, 'barely out of the nursery when the iniquitous bargain was made between the parents.' (The bargain was in settlement of some debt.) But Carn Cross had already lost his heart to a Miss Maunsell of Limerick. He died less than a year after his marriage, in 1801, at Youghal where his regiment was quartered, and Miss Maunsell had the melancholy satisfaction of erecting an altar tomb to his memory in the graveyard of St Mary's Church.

His brother, John James, grandfather of Susan Mitchell, was a courtly and arresting personality, versed in law, who rose rapidly to success. According to his daughter, he was appointed Barrackmaster of Sligo at the age of 15. He was educated at Portora, and perhaps at Castleknock for a time. He joined the army on January 31, 1799 and is later mentioned as being on the strength of the Leitrim Militia, though he had not yet arrived from the 2nd Battalion of Light Infantry. He had joined his regiment by 1800, with a salary of £14. 11. 11d. a month and he was soon to be promoted to the rank of major, though he remained on captain's pay until the end of the year. This was while Carn Cross was still a captain. The regiment moved about from Naas, to Waterford, and then to Youghal.

As the colonel of the regiment was attending Parliament, John James Cullen – a young man of 18 – acted as commanding officer, signing the muster sheets with the flourish of his initials and surname. It was he who had to sign the muster sheets in which his 19 old brother, Carn Cross, is entered as being ill and then again when he was dead.

Throughout 1802, the regiment moved about, from Youghal to Dungarvan, Lismore, Cappoquin, Roscrea, Thurles and Carrick-on-Shannon. John James acted as commanding officer on and off during the next few years, being stationed at Carlow, Athy, Avoca, the Curragh Camp, Roscrea and Bantry. On May 25, 1806, he was promoted to the rank of Lieutenant-Colonel,[6] and so became second-in-command in the regiment. By now his salary was £24. 13. 5d a month. He had permission to act as High Sheriff of County Leitrim in 1807. He also spent some time recruiting as the regiment moved about.

Apart from his military activities, John James Cullen was very conscious of his role as head of the Cullen family. His brother had had a son posthumously, another Carn Cross – known as Carney Cullen. Carney's mother had remarried, a Reverend Herbert Mandeville Nash, who, Kate Mitchell notes caustically in her memoir, 'feathered his nest very comfortably on the pickings of the Minor and therewith built a whole row of houses in Bundoran'. John James, with his sound sense, was responsible for much of the arrangement of affairs in the family but did not approve of the union. Now he himself, at the age of 27, decided to marry.

His bride was one of the Finucanes of County Clare. They traced their ancestry back to Morgan Finucane in the early 16th century. Descendants two centuries after him had conformed to the Established Church. Bridget was the eldest daughter of Daniel Finucane, of Stamer Park, in Ennis. Her mother, Catherine Daxon, of Fountain which is also in Clare, was the sister of Giles Daxon, who married a Miss White – 'a very plain woman, but had a large fortune'. Giles himself lives on in the pages of Charles Lever's *Harry Lorrequer* as one of the notable characters in the Dublin of his day.[7]

Giles Daxon had no family, so he had adopted his niece, Bridget (known as Bidz), giving her a good education. Petite and dark, with brilliant eyes, Bidz was married from his house in Kildare Street, Dublin, in 1810, when she was 17, with a fortune of £3000 and a present of a handsome carriage. The wedding took place, as was fashionable then, in the house. The affianced

---

6. According to the official Army List, Sir H. Macanelley, *History of the Irish Militia*, 1949, notes the date of promotion as May 30, 1808. I am grateful to Pádraig Ó Snodaigh for drawing my attention to this point.

7. At the beginning of Chapter 39, O'Leary is astonished that Trevanion has never heard the story of the Knight of Kerry and Billy M'Cabe.
    ' "Then maybe you never knew Giles Daxon?"
    "I have not that pleasure either."
    "Lord bless me . . . I thought he was better known than the Duke of Wellington or the travelling piper." '
    The novel, *Harry Lorequer*, was first published in 1839.

couple presided at a dinner party in the evening. Among their guests was the Bishop of Kilmore, Dr Beresford, who, when dinner was over, married them in the drawing room. After that there was a celebratory ball and the new husband and wife spent what remained of the night in Kildare Street.

The muster sheets of the Leitrim Militia record the Lieutenant-Colonel as being on leave from September to December in 1810 and 'absent without leave' for most of 1811, when he and his wife would have been visiting various relatives around the west and north-west of Ireland, and perhaps seeing to the affairs of Skreeney where John James's mother, Ellen, still lived. Carney, his nephew who was heir to Skreeney, and nearly 10 years of age, was growing up with a dislike of the place.

The regiment moved to Canterbury in December 1811, and John James – Bidz accompanying him – was recruiting from then until March 1812, when they moved to Bristol with the regiment for the rest of the year. By March 1813, they were back in Ireland once more, moving about from Cavan to Belturbet, Boyle, Carrick-on-Shannon and Nenagh. In November 1814, the regiment was 'disembodied'. With the peace of 1815, and the end of the

Lieutenant-Colonel John James Cullen (1783-1842), 1821, by Martin Cregan (1788-1870). Private collection, Dublin. (Photograph courtesy of Fergus Pyle.)

Bidz Finucane Cullen (1783-1861), 1821, by Martin Cregan (1788-1870). Private collection, Dublin. (Photograph courtesy of Fergus Pyle.)

Napoleonic threat, all the militia regiments were disbanded, and John James Cullen was presented with a handsome silver salver, costing 100 guineas, by his fellow officers and the non-commissioned officers of his regiment.

The records observe that he continued to be paid 'by agent' until the end of 1816. But Lieutenant-Colonel Cullen now settled down to the life of a country gentleman. No more would he be mocked by the locals when he entered a country town with his men –

> In Enniskillen I was bred
> Free from debt and danger,
> Till Colonel Cullen listed me
> To be a Barony Ranger.[8]

---

8. Victoria Diana Franklin (née Mitchell, youngest daughter of Kate Cullen) to her sister Jinny Mitchell, n.d. She heard the ballad quoted by a Mr Gaffney of Sligo c. 1911.

Already he and his wife had three children, and by 1832, when Kate appeared, Bidz would have borne him 12 more, of whom three died in infancy. John James Cullen and his wife, like his parents before him, were considered to be an outstandingly handsome couple. When the Prince Regent – 'on whose moral character we will not touch', interpolates Kate severely in her narrative – made his grand entry as the newly crowned King into Dublin, the Cullens were there to celebrate with the rest and had their portraits painted to commemorate the occasion. Martin Cregan, the fashionable portrait painter of the day, showed the Lieutenant-Colonel in his dress uniform – an arresting figure. A dark man, his supercilious eyebrows in a wide forehead are balanced by a firm mouth. The dynamic Bidz wears a huge ostrich feather, probably what she had worn for the Levée in Dublin Castle, and a cameo on her wrist. Both were bright-eyed, with aristocratic noses.

John James rented Skreeney from his nephew, Carney Cullen, who was growing up an eccentric, and who 'from fear of being annoyed by the ghosts of his ancestors eschewed living in the family place.' Rejection, or dislike, of the past transmitted itself to Carney's only son, from whom he was eventually estranged. According to Kate, her cousin's 'series of follies culminated in his publicly declaring himself a Roman Catholic and espousing the cause of the Fenians': and thus came the breach with his father. Carney and his son, in the eyes of the rest of the family, were totally extravagant, and between them managed to squander a good inheritance. Their entire property was sold in the Encumbered Estates Court shortly after Carney's death, and the premature death of his son, in the late 1870s.

Before this, however, when Carney Cullen had come of age and abhorred Skreeney, he had built himself a fine Georgian villa, about four miles from Manorhamilton, on the road to Bundoran, under the majestic shadow of Ben Bulben. The single storey building, with steps up to the colonnaded portico, is there still, pathetically dignified in its surroundings of rhododendrons and neglected trees, the pediment of the facade surmounted by the crest of the pelican in her nest, feeding her young. The family motto was 'Carpe diem' – 'enjoy the day' (or alternatively – as John James might have put it – 'don't waste time'!)

Carney had married one of his cousins, Jane Palmer of Shriff. They had six daughters, as well as the single miscreant son and seem to have had little to do with their Cullen cousins at Skreeney, though Kate records them and their misfortunes along with the brief histories of her other numerous relatives. When Carney's son was born, three-year-old red-tufted Kate was chosen to be the emissary of the congratulations from Skreeney. A tiny note on pink satin paper, in Bidz's handwriting, survives among the family papers. 'A Coral & Balls, from Catharine Theresa Cullen, to her pretty little Cousin Carn Cross Cullen, of Glenade, with a Thousand loves and kisses. Skreeney August 31st, 1835'.

Carney Cullen's house at Glenade. (Author's photograph.)

Carney's mother-in-law, Kate Palmer, was John James's eldest sister. Like her unfortunate elder brother, Carn Cross, she had been fated to confront her stern father when it came to matrimony. She, however, dealt with matters differently.

Captain Palmer, who was quartered at Sligo in the Prince of Wales's Fencibles, proposed for her hand, but the Reverend Carn Cross would not hear of the match. The captain's origins were obscure.

> However, 'Faint heart never won fair Lady' and the young lady in question being on a visit with her Aunt Mrs Manley at Auburn (the hill at Auburn is still called by the country people 'Manley's Brae') near the town of Sligo, eloped one night with her Captain bold, getting over a wall by a ladder. A horse provided with a pillion was waiting with the lover, and, seated behind him, she rode 27 miles to Boyle, where they were married, by a dis-frocked parson; but the Revd. Carney followed them and married them over again himself.'

The Palmers lived in Shriff, at Dromahaire, on the Sligo-Leitrim border, and had a family of one son and five daughters. All were handsome and attractive, but, in Kate's opinion, with a mother totally unfit to govern them, they were wayward and did not turn out well. 'Old Captain Palmer', she comments, 'was a worthless man, selfish, always in an impecunious condition, hiding from creditors and evading them'.

> He once got himself arrested while walking with my father in Dublin, knowing that he would pay the debt, which was a tailor's bill. His practice was to periodically visit England, having first scraped together all the money he could get, which he manfully spent at some English watering place, not that he either drank or gambled, but he liked to live in comfort and without the cares of a family.

It was John James who continually came to Kate Palmer's rescue, with a regular cart of provisions sent from Skreeney. He had two other sisters and a younger brother, Henry Francis, who was a Captain in the Leitrim Militia, and retired to Rockwood, a plain house, a few miles from Skreeney. Henry was a gentle amiable man, handsome like his brother, with a family of 11 children. But he had married unhappily, his wife, a 'very unprincipled virago', being a niece of the Miss Dickson whom his and John James's eldest brother Carn Cross had been compelled to marry.

Aunt Hessie was very good-looking, but very untidy, and an absolute bully. Kate's mother, Bidz, remembered visiting the Dicksons' home at Woodville during her bridal tour, and

> going upstairs one night she saw a beautiful lady kneeling at her bed, saying her prayers, her long black hair hanging down over her white dressing-gown. This lady was Aunt Hessie's mother, Mrs Dixon [sic]. She was one of the Bodkins of Galway, commonly known as the 'bloody Bodkins'. They were Roman Catholics, but my aunt Hessie was not a very strict member of that faith, but always went to Manorhamilton Church that she might refresh her eyes with whatever was to be seen, and hear the week's gossip from the Skreeneyites or the Glenades.

John James's sister Jane also lived near Skreeney, in a cottage he had built for her and her husband on Colonel Sam Whyte's property (John James acted as agent to Colonel Whyte). Aunt Jane had married a Captain Gledstanes in the Donegal Militia, who belonged to a good family in Tyrone, and was reputed to be well off, but his father was extravagant, and had persuaded Uncle George, when he came of age, to sign some paper which made him liable for all the debts which the old man had contracted.

For some years, the aging couple had struggled to keep on their house in Tyrone – Daisy Hill – which Aunt Jane managed to perfection, but they were obliged to place it in the hands of a receiver, and come to Manorhamilton to enjoy the generosity of her brother. They were popular at Skreeney.

'Aunt Jane . . . surpassed everyone I ever knew in knowing how to do everything better than anyone else,' wrote Kate in her memoir. 'No one could beat her in cookery, dairy work (oh! such butter and cream!!), such preserves, such cakes, such pastry, I can taste them yet. To spend a day at Lisnagro was the greatest treat we as youngsters could get, especially when the strawberries were ripe, for Uncle George was famous as a strawberry grower.'

Some of Aunt Jane's ways

> were a little peculiar, in particular I can remember her devotional habits, which she always carried out with rigid exactness, the daily perusal of so many chapters of the Bible, and the repetition of so many prayers, some of this for evening was got through before dinner, and the rest after dinner. I well recollect when she used to stay at Skreeney, she would bring me upstairs with her to stay with her 'till she had finished her prayers'; this would occur even if there was a party going on, and I think she sometimes used to fall asleep and I was often kept much longer than I bargained for. On returning to the drawing-room, should my Uncle George have joined the ladies, she was sure to be greeted with, 'Well Jane, I hope you have had a good sleep', but the bantering had no effect, she steadily pursued her plan of devotion to the last.

Eliza, John James's youngest sister, was quite a contrast with Aunt Jane. She married an elderly Major Jones of the 9th Lancers when a young girl, and they sailed for India, leaving their first child, Eliza, with her grandmother at Skreeney. There they had a second daughter, Jemima, and a few years later Major Jones died.

Eliza, a much admired beauty, was haughty and imperious. She could unbend, and make herself fascinating, when she pleased and the young officers of the regiment adored her. After the death of Major Jones, she decided to come home with her daughter, and took a passage in an East Indiaman.

> A young officer of the Regt. was also coming home, a Mr Campbell. He also took his passage in that ship for the pleasure of travelling in company with Mrs Jones. When my aunt heard this she changed to another ship.

> Mr Campbell, determined to carry his point, also changed, and so fate settled that they should travel together, and, whatever way they managed matters, when the vessel put in at St Helena they went on shore together and got married.

> Meanwhile, the friends at home having received letters from her filled with the most extravagant expressions of grief for the Major, in one of which she said 'he died in my arms and left me miserable for ever'! were rather surprised to hear of the arrival of a bride instead of, as they had anticipated, a disconsolate widow.

The people of those days were fiery and impulsive, and my Grandmother was so scandalised at her haste in so soon making a second marriage that she vowed she would not let her enter Skreeney. However, my father induced her to change her mind, and, after much persuasion and much strong letter writing, she at last received them.

Mr Campbell, a reserved, quiet man, soon found he had acquired a tartar, who ruled him with a rod of iron. Aunt Eliza showed the greatest indifference towards her two daughters by her first husband, so kind Aunt Jane adopted the elder one, and the younger girl, Jemima, was brought up by her stepfather's mother, who was astonished at how her own mother neglected her.

Such were Kate Cullen's near relatives, gathered in the vicinity of Skreeney, the family home, within easy reach of Sligo. They give a reasonable cross-section of the types of Anglo-Irish gentry at the beginning of the 19th century, who enjoyed both privilege and responsibility. The gentle Mr Campbell was soon to become Colonel and then Brigadier-General of his regiment. He died in 1849.

Aunt Eliza Campbell had nothing to do with the Skreeney Cullens after the death of John James a few years before that. However, Kate adds wryly, 'I believe she carried on a correspondence with the Cullens of Glenade, from whom she obtained all the information she wanted about the family.'

2

Bid Old Days Return

Skreeney c.1815-1840

Kate Cullen had nothing but admiration for her father.

> My dear Father is the great central figure in the memories of my child-
> hood, and stands out in never fading clearness as if I had seen him but
> yesterday; he was a typical Irish gentleman of that day, a grand pres-
> ence, genial manners, and I have never seen him surpassed in the greeting
> of his guests.

> On entering his drawing room before dinner, he conversed well and was
> often humorous. His tastes were refined and he always liked to be
> surrounded with pretty things, the books of the day, china, and all
> articles of vertu, pictures, engravings, etc., he was always gathering
> about him. He took great pride in the old family place, and had it always
> in beautiful order, on the trees and shrubs he bestowed special care, and
> many trees are standing there now which he planted.

On leaving the regiment, John James maintained the Skreeney property, as
well as several large agencies in the County, the principal one belonging to
Mr Luke Whyte, whose son would become Lord Annaly. Luke Whyte had
started life as a pedlar, standing on Carlisle Bridge in Dublin,[1] with a tray of
old books suspended by a strap around his neck, and he made his fortune
from a lottery ticket which he found in one of these books. Grandmother
Finucane had often seen Whyte on Carlisle Bridge, and, meeting him afterwards at dinner at Skreeney, pronounced him 'a most polished finished
gentleman! as if 'quite to the manner born'.

John James had his troubles. He had been doing much to improve his
own property in the neighbourhood of the old Castle. A draft letter survives
from November 1823, in which he makes representation to Lord Leitrim
about the tenure of some fields in Manorhamilton, attached to land originally
belonging to the Algeo family. His uncle, the late Major Cullen, had obtained
the lease of the tenement and a small garden on which he had laid out nearly
£1000 and John James, who inherited it, had been making a profit of £30 a

---

1. Now O'Connell Bridge.

year from rents, until times had deteriorated. Now he felt he could no longer let the property without the adjoining fields, which his father had improved by planting trees. But Mr Algeo refused to sign the necessary papers.

Young Kate, known affectionately by the family as Kitzy, knew nothing at the time of local tensions among the gentry and she was naturally sheltered from the growing land problems of the period. However Skreeney, while not a remarkable building, left a luxuriant imprint on her mind. It was her home for the first 10 years of her life. Now no longer standing, it can be recreated in the imagination from her vivid description.

> Skreeney was an old-fashioned country house, the shape of an 'L'. It had a long hall as you went in, off which was the drawing-room, facing the hall-door, my father's study to the left showing two windows.

(She does not mention the travelling library, standing in the study, which still survives in the family. A handsome, sturdy and compact mahogany bookcase, like a box, with brass handles and discreet doors, it would have fed the Lt Colonel's mind as he moved about the country recruiting. The range of books – Smollett, Shakespeare, Cowper, Fielding and Racine among the authors – is an adequate measure of his cultivated interests.)

To the front of the house was the girls' schoolroom, beyond which lay the garden 'of the old-fashioned type',

> Where were long beds full of evening primroses and crimson 'Burgundy' and pale yellow double primroses and white, and bunches of Columbine in purple and pink, also dwarf plants of the ever-blowing rose. The walk through this little garden terminated at the river which came down from the wood roaring into the yard, and continued its course through the domain under a little bridge, where was the 'Green Gate'.

Elsewhere she revels in the old-fashioned garden, divided into squares by laurel and beech hedges, 'with oceans of Lily of the Valley, Daffodils, Narcissus, double white and yellow Primroses and Pansies in the Spring, and in the Summer Roses everywhere, and a wealth of the common fruits'. These included Scarlet Crofton, balring and pear trees and peach apples.

> On the lawn in front of the house was a beautiful holly tree – a lovely object when in full berry: on from that was a ditch known as the Ha-ha: and on the top of this were some walnut trees of some age and very fine shrubs, bearing generally a good crop of walnuts which were seldom touched till the coming of Halloweve. There were also Portugal laurels with their pretty white blossoms resembling somewhat laurestinus.

> The garden lay to the left of the house, a little to the back in the

Page of manuscript memoir. Private collection, Dublin.

direction of the back road which brought you to a small town called Garrison. On each side of this road was a thick belt of trees called the wood. Going along this road you passed the 'Foggy Hill Fort' with its double ditch.

But back to the house.

'Come on through the long hall', Kate writes, 'where were three windows with delightful seats.

> This was a great playground on wet days. The diningroom was to the right of the hall: it had two high windows, the walls were painted a deep pink, and on them were hung the family portraits, my Grandfather and Grandmother, Madame Knox, Mrs Shugal leaning her head on her hand (a most melancholy-looking person having been crossed in love). My Uncle Major Frank of the Prince of Wales's Fencibles, in his red coat; Colonel John Wynne (of General Cathcart's Regiment of Dragoons, my maternal great-grand uncle).

(No wonder Carney had been nervous of family ghosts.)

To this gallery of departed persons was added the pair of portraits painted by Cregan, Kate's father, and her mother, known locally as 'the little lady

Mrs. Shugal 'crossed in love'. Artist unknown. Private collection, Dublin.
(Photograph courtesy of Fergus Pyle.)

from Clare'.[2] Carn Cross Cullen of Glenade was something of an artist himself, seemingly, because he had copies of these portraits made for Glenade
House by a Mr Nelson who, according to Kate, received his first lessons in
painting from Carney; and his daughter Hester later presented these to Kate.[3]

A list of the family plate made by John James in August 1820, with
additions in 1822, quotes the value at over £300. There were candlesticks,
candlebranches, chased and fiddlehandled table and dessert spoons, crested
soup ladles, wine casters, a silver cream ewer, salvers, bread baskets, a marrow
scoop and a round-of-beef skewer: which calls up a picture of sparkling
parties while the children were growing up, entertaining family friends and –
later – prospective suitors for the elder daughters.

The memoir moves on to the drawing room.

> The drawing-room looked out on the back lawn, which went up a hill,
> where was a magnificent silver fir and some walnut trees, which bore
> fruit every year. Three bow windows formed the back of the drawing-
> room.
>
> In the middle window was a crimson covered sofa where my Mother
> often rested after a tiring day. The Carpet was crimson, brown and
> drab; the chimneypiece of good Marble, grey and white with a pattern
> of looped wreaths in relief. The old Cabinet (Japanese) stood against the
> wall. My Father bought it in the street in Bristol when his Regiment
> was quartered there. He got the stand made for it and it was all painted
> and done up in its original style by Anna Patten, sister of Francis Cullen
> of Corry [first cousin of John James], who was an expert in this kind of
> work. . . .
>
> Four engravings called the 'Four Ages'[4] hung round the walls of the
> Drawing-room, also the 'Lord of the Vineyard' and the 'French and
> English Firesides' (red). In the 'English Fireside', the gentlemen were
> represented as standing with their backs to the fire while the ladies
> shivered in the background, while in the 'French Fireside' the ladies
> take the best places in front of the fire, and their Cavaliers are very glad
> to hang on the backs of their chairs and catch any ray of heat that may
> come their way.
>
> The piano – a 'Grand' one, which had been bought at an auction at
> Lord Lorton's (or some of the King family) and had been a good one in

---

2.   According to Kate's grandson, Michael Franklin, who heard it from his mother, Victoria
     Diana Franklin.
3.   The original Cregan portraits went to Jemmy Cullen, one of Kate's brothers.
4.   *Les Quatres Ages de l'Homme* by Jean Raoux (1677 1734), engraved by Jean Moyreau
     (1690 1762). 1. L'Enfance. 2. La Jeunesse. 3. L'Age Viril. 4. La Vieillesse.

Detail of 'L'Age Viril' from Les Quatre Ages de l'Homme by Jean Raoux (1677–1734), engraved by Jean Moyreau (1690–1762). Private collection, Dublin. (Photograph courtesy of Fergus Pyle.)

its day, and done good service, and was still in fair order, considering its years – was most used at this period, during the courtship of my sister Bessie and her fiancé Noblett St Leger, who belonged to a very musical family, and sang himself in a pleasing manner.

A small railed table of dark mahogany with carved legs – a card-table covered with green cloth, which folded up and had very spidery legs, round which were played 'Brag', 'Loo', 'Commerce' and 'Beggar my Neighbour' by the young ones in the evenings – all these pieces of furniture are indelibly impressed on my memory as having been the objects of my childish admiration, and the Laughter echoing from the card-table is still ringing in my ears.[5]

Kate, in her reminiscences, takes the reader on a guided tour of the vanished house, starting next towards the staircase.

Near the Dining-room door, two flights of stairs led up to the nursery and the maid's room. Between these two rooms was a mysterious Staircase commonly known as the 'Cats' Stairs', which led up to two large rooms, the precise use of which was never known, but they were used in my time entirely as lumber-rooms and were full of trunks, and these stairs were much frequented by cats – hence the name.

By the front staircase one ascended to my mother's room. At the head of that stairs was my father's dressing-room, which he was in the habit of giving up to any gentleman visitor who had a valet. The valet slept there to be within call of his master, who would probably sleep in the Green Room next door.

Ascending five or six steps further were my Mother's bedroom and the Red Room. My Father's dressing-room, I should mention was known as the stair-head-closet, and in it stood my Father's chest of drawers, known as the Tall Boy.

My Mother's bedroom was a large room over the drawing-room, and in it stood my Mother's bed, a four poster curtained all round. My bed was at the foot of the four poster, and was a little low green bed with a patchwork quilt. If I was frightened in the night, I made a practice of creeping over the foot to my Mother who used to tuck me into the curtain.

Jemmy, seven years older than herself and a great favourite with her mother

---

5. The drawing–room of such happy memories, according to a manuscript note among the family papers, measured 24 ft with the bow of the window (and 21 ft without) by 4½ yds. The measurements of the dining parlour were 19½ ft the length, its breadth 17½ ft.

– Kate secretly believed this ruined him for future life – slept in the corner of the room, in a bed with blue curtains, with a comfortable nightcap tied under his chin, and Aunt Jane used to come at night to gossip over the fire with her sister-in-law, until Father came up.

Like the drawing-room, this bedroom had three good windows. Next door was a room called the Boudoir – formerly used by Patrick Cullen's wife, Judith Wynne, as a dressing-room. She was remembered by the family as 'the lady that drained the rushy bottom in her husband's absence to make a lake there', so cutting off the cattle's water supply.

During Kitzy's childhood in the 1830s, her sisters Georgina and Diana slept in the Boudoir, and sat up very late at night. 'Burning too many candles, which action of theirs had to be looked into and stopped.' Many girls stayed in the house, crowding in the Boudoir at night, gossiping about their lovers, including the two Palmer cousins, Mary Anne and Susan – very different from their father, Kate considered, the impecunious captain 'who had none of the pleasant old fashioned ways, 'the little grey man' having brought all the English trash into that family.'

On the same staircase flight was the Red Room, slept in by visiting in-laws, and having a good 'modern' mahogany bed. Between the Red Room and the Green Room was the china closet, where china and glass for special use was kept. The nurse and nursery maid slept in the nursery.

> The children had their breakfasts there, and they got bread dipped in cream. Diana at one time took on herself to give it out, telling Anne Toler, the nurse, not to trouble to get up, as she would leave the children's bread on their saucers. She dipped her own slice first, and put it away, getting the cream of the cream. She afterwards told this story against herself, and it was said that until the age of 12 years, she had a snub nose, but that all the cream she purloined made a bridge to it, and indeed she had one of the most perfectly shaped noses I have ever seen.

A short flight of stairs led from their mother's bedroom to the 'Barrack room', where the boys other than Jemmy slept, Carn Cross (the 'Minor'), Johnny Marcus, Paddy and Francis, who was two years older than Kate, and her constant companion. Any stray young men, on a visit 'for the shooting etc.', slept in the Barrack room.

'In the school-room downstairs we had tea every night', Kate remembered. This was presided over by Janey, who was eight years older than Kitzy, and the youngest of her sisters. Janey was prim and something of an old maid.

> My father's tea was carried into him in the Dining-room by me and James; I carrying thin bread and butter and Jemmy the tea: the bread and butter was, I think, cut by Gorman in the Pantry before tea. The

58

Wisdom the wine merchant, very precious. Of Labatt at this time it might be said "He was a great man and I have forgotten all his faults." He never did anything unkind to me nor said an offensive word in my presence. The nurse and nurserymaid slept in the nursery. The children had their breakfasts there and they got bread dipped in cream, Diana at one time took on herself to give it out telling Anne Toler the nurse not to trouble to get up as she would leave the children's bread on their saucers. She dipped her own slice first & put it away getting the cream of the cream. She afterwards told this story against herself & it was said that until the age of 12 years she had a snub nose but that all the cream she purloined made a bridge to it, and indeed she had one of the most perfectly shaped noses I have ever seen. From my mother's bedroom door a short flight of stairs led to the "Barrack Room" where the rest of the boys slept — the "minor",

Page of manuscript memoir, with Susan Mitchell's handwriting followed by text in Kate Cullen Mitchell's hand. Private collection, Dublin.

boys, who had been banished from the civilised part of the house to have their smoke in Gorman's pantry (smoking not being allowed in the other rooms – I never saw my Father smoke), appeared at the tea, also my Mother and the girls and whatever Governess was there at the time.

Tea consisted of tea, bread and butter, varied by jam on special occasions. Toast was sometimes allowed to be made at the school room fire. I was supposed to be packed off to bed at 9 o'clock, and if anything amusing was going on, tears usually accompanied the exodus!

Those who were old enough to remain up later generally played chess or cards, or did fancy-work . . . (Berlin wool-work was introduced about this time) till bedtime. Company being in the house, all sat in the drawing-room, and music went on. Georgina sang, and Bessie and Diana played. Paddy could also sing a very good song and had a nice voice. My Father sometimes displayed the contents of the old cabinet, which were very interesting, to visitors. He also had many nice books: annuals bound in silk, which was a fashion in that day. The names of these were 'The Amulet', 'Bijou', 'Keepsake' etc.

When I grew older, I was allowed to sit up to listen to the music on these occasions. I would wear a white muslin frock with low neck and short sleeves, and made with little capes on the shoulders, and a sash of blue, pink or plaid ribbon, which was generally obtained at [the] Miss Faussetts' of Sligo, dear old ladies, friends of ours, who owing to the extravagance of their father were obliged to open a shop, and were greatly respected by the country gentry, and visited and patronised by all.

The evening for me . . . concluded with prayers in the schoolroom, which were generally read by my Father, my brother Paddy, when at home, reading the epistles in his beautiful, deep voice, by which I shall always remember him.

In the morning, a short prayer was read before breakfast, from a prayer-book called 'Swete's Prayers'. Then after breakfast (which consisted of stirabout, hot bread, eggs, cold meat etc.), at about 11 o'clock, my Father read the Psalms and Lessons for the day in the School-room. Luncheon was at 2 o'c in the Dining-room; it consisted of Potatoes and butter and a large jug of milk, and cold meat was placed on the side-board. This was the children's dinner, and they sat at their own table at the side of the room. Dinner was at 6 o'clock, sometimes in summer at 5, and when there were visitors tea and coffee were brought into the Drawing-room by the Butler – Gorman – after dinner, and poured out by one of the girls, Diana or Janey perhaps.

So normal life passed by pleasantly for the younger children, unaware of what was happening in the outside world. The older ones were being drawn into it. In July of 1828, before Kitzy was born, Bessie who was 14 wrote to her 15 year-old sister, Mary (John James's eldest daughter) from Ennis. Bessie was staying at Stamer Park with Grandmother Finucane, who had adopted their second eldest brother Giles (named after Great-Uncle Giles Daxon, their mother's guardian, from whose house in Dublin Bidz had been married). Ennis town was in a ferment of excitement, because Daniel O'Connell and his supporters had arrived to contest Vesey Fitzgerald for the County Clare election.

Bessie wrote:

> The town was crowded to excess for the last few days. Mrs George O'Callaghan came to town for the week. She lodged at the last house on the causeway. We used to go there every day, and see the people coming in in parties with green flags and two Priests at their heads.

Daniel O'Connell – as one of 'The O'Connell Triumvirate' ('Honest Jack' Lawless (1773-1887), Daniel O'Connell (1775-1847) and Richard Lalor Sheil (1791-1851)) by John Doyle ('HB'), 1830.
(Photograph courtesy of the National Gallery of Ireland, no. 2082.)

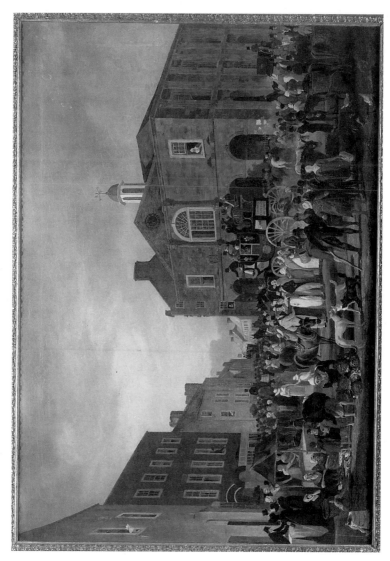

The Marketplace at Ennis, c.1820, by William Turner de Lond. Knight of Glin collection.
(Photograph courtesy of the Courtauld Institute of Art, London.)

Carmodys hotel been opposite, when O Connel stopt we had a full view of what O Connels people were doing. There was a bust of O Connel which came down from Dublin and it was always in the window at Carmodys so we had a full view of him. There was a platform erected outside Mrs Flins Drawing room window where O Connel his son Lawless Steel [*i.e.* Sheil] [and] Maguire from our Country used to speak.

When Lawless came out to speak he told us that as St Paul spoke to the Galatians he Jack Lawless spoke to the Forty Shilling Freeholders. The races begun last Saturday with everyone out the first day but the election beginning on Monday the people were afraid to go. There were to have been two ball during the week but they even were put off. . . .

This country is in a very alarming state. There was a man killed about six miles from this the other night. There was a large [crowd] of Roman Catholics assembled who were disputing. And the man who was killed, when he came out, come, said they, let us have a blow at the Protestant rascal. They got him down and killed him on the spot.[6]

Bessie writes with a strong, mature hand. The Cullens, whether boys or girls, were educated well, by private tutors and governesses, some of the boys going on afterwards to public school.

Mary Jane, the eldest sister, was gentle, with a social conscience. In November of that year she married the local curate, the Reverend Edward Labatt, whose father, Kate – with her literary turn – noted, was immortalised by Samuel Lover. Dr Samuel Bell Labatt was famous in Dublin for founding His Majesty's Cow-Pock Institution in Sackville Street and Kate's mother was the first person to introduce this form of vaccination into Leitrim. Kate quotes stories about Edward's mother.

Dr Samuel's wife was a person who played a prominent part among the servants of Dublin of that day, being known amongst them as 'Lock-Pot', on account of putting a padlock on her Soup-pot or Digester, so as to frustrate any intended assaults upon it. I often had the honour when a child of driving about with her in her chariot. She had been something of a beauty in her day, and had, I think, 27 children. Edward was the eldest . . . Lock-Pot's flirtations were well known in Dublin, and were the subject of many a jest at dinner-parties. Her family called her 'Jane'. 'Jane weep!' said her son Jonathan on the occasion of her husband's death, when it was said she wept. 'Jane weep! It would take a miracle like Saul of Tarsus to make Jane weep!'

---

6. Bessie Cullen to Mary Jane Cullen, July 29, 1828.

Edward Labatt proposed for Mary when she was only 14. But John James, who did not care for him, insisted on them waiting for a year, and Mary was packed off with her mother to the relatives in Clare. There, because of her beauty, she was made much of, and she received another proposal from a county gentleman of means. She still preferred Labatt, and married him at 15 and the marriage, according to Kate, was not a happy one. John James would have liked her to return home to Skreeney, but Mary never left her husband. He soon tired of her, says Kate. 'He was a regular tyrant, and by no means a good man in a moral point of view. It would be neither edifying nor interesting to state here the actions of this bad man', Kate pronounces severely, though, elsewhere in her narrative, she admits that he was a great support after the death of her father.[7]

John James was writing to his wife, in 1830, expressing his dissatisfaction with Labatt. Bidz was on a visit to her family in Stamer Park, in Ennis, and the Labatts were in Dublin. 'I have not heard a word of or from Edwd. Labatt', exploded John James to Bidz. 'I wrote to him last week to beg he would not forget to pay his Bills in the bank, which will fall due early next month & to give him my opinion as to his trip to Town and the object of it. He has never replied to me'.[8]

Later that year Bidz's brother, Michael Finucane, hoped that Labatt might get the living of Ennis. 'It is worth over six hundred a year and nothing to do we have I am sorry to say so fine protestants', he commented sarcastically.[9] But Labatt eventually went to a parish in Donegal, and became private chaplain to the Earl of Enniskillen.

Kitzy, born in 1832, was familiar with Manorhamilton Church in the late 1830s, after the Labatts had moved to Donegal, and there were two new curates.

> On Sundays we all went to Church in an inside car, which we called the 'tub', a vehicle very commonly used in domains where there were children, as it was supposed to be safer than any other kind, a thick leather apron being buttoned across which kept off the rain and prevented the small children from falling out. The boys who had attained the ages of 10 or 11 preferred going across the fields, and probably reached the

---

7.   There was a second curate of Manorhamilton Union at the same time as Labatt, a George D. Crooke, whose grandson – it is interesting to observe in this account of the enclosed socity of 19th century Protestants – became engaged to Kitzy's daughter Susan sixty years later. George Crooke's three children were born and baptised in Manorhamilton before his premature death. Susan met the eldest, Milward, after he had retired to Birr, and she became intimate with his children, all about her own age. Her fiancé was George Douglas Crooke, 1865–1897.

8.   John James Cullen to Bidz Cullen, March 31, 1830.

9.   Michael Finucane to Bidz Cullen, March 31, 1830.

church first, crossing a stile and getting in by the back of the church.

The church was as handsome and plain within as it was outside, a simple rectangle, with a gallery added later above the west door. It is a wide, high interior, lit with four plain glass gothic windows on each side. The chancel is raised, and reached by a few steps, windows on each side. The Cullen family pew was in the chancel, behind the small wooden pulpit. With the choir opposite them they were removed from the remainder of the congregation.

The Henry Cullens, of Rockwood, also attended Manorhamilton Church, and sometimes the Cullens of Glenade, though they tended to go to Kinloch – 'considering it more fashionable'. The vicar, Kate recalls, was the Reverend Abraham Hamilton, uncle of John Hamilton, one of the curates, who later married her cousin Minnie, third daughter of Carney Cullen of Glenade.

> John Hamilton had red hair, and was called by the children 'the cat', as he was supposed to ressemble this animal, and the other curate, Atthill, was named 'the dog', as he had black curly hair and was considered like a King Charles black-and-tan.

> My father usually handed the plate, and in his absence Johnny Marcus or some of the other boys took his place, or Uncle George Gledstanes. He and my Aunt Jane sat in the corner seats of the Skreeney pew, also Eliza Webb and her two little children. 'Are you coming up to lunch, George? Indeed you may as well stay to dinner as the St Legers are here'. 'Oh no thank you, John, I'm beginning the mowing to-morrow, and I must see about the men, as it's getting late in the month'. My Aunt Jane upon this gave a private sign to my Mother, that she would like to come as Bessie was there, and not to mind George, and they invariably came in the end. This little dialogue, with variations, took place every Sunday on coming out of church; and it became a laughing matter as we always knew that Uncle George intended to come all the time.

On particular occasions, such as the Sunday of the special sermon preached in aid of the Protestant orphans, the plate was handed round by Kitzy's mother, and Mrs Algeo of Glenboy.

> They took different sides, attended – my mother by Col. Armstrong, and Mrs Algeo by my uncle George, as esquires. The Skreeney silver salvers were sent down to Blair, the Sexton, for this purpose. As each pew was collected from, the contents of the salver were emptied into the church poor-box, which was held by my Uncle George at one side, and by Col. Armstrong at the other. . . .

> The church is now greatly altered . . . I think I heard it has now a

seraphine or harmonium, or other abomination: my recollection is Irwin
the clerk and his son sitting under the reading desk, droning out the
psalms with the usual nasal twang.

Another memory, dating from when she was nine, was of the visit of
Father Mathew to Glenfarne Chapel, not far from Manorhamilton. Her father, and all the boys, went to hear him preach, and they were gratified to be
introduced to him. All the servants, including Gorman the butler, who was
fond of his liquor, went too, and took the pledge – 'and kept it for some time.'
Gorman, in fact, had already promised John James that he would not take any
drink unless it was handed to him by one of the family. It was a family joke
that Gorman would hand a hat to one of the boys, saying, 'Feel that now,
Master Paddy, how heavy it is. Now hand it back to me.' The hat, of course,
hid a full bottle of whiskey.

A visitor to Skreeney, on two or three occasions, was the old bishop of
Kilmore, John Claudius Beresford, a great friend of Kate's father.

> My Father one day drove the Bishop over to Glencar to see the Water-
> fall. I am not sure if it was on this occasion or another that he said to
> him, 'I've got a salmon from Bundrowse for your dinner to-morrow, my
> Lord'. 'Is it crimped,[10] John?' replied his Lordship, 'for if it isn't it
> won't be worth a damn!' Whether the reply to this was in the affirma-
> tive or negative, I cannot say.

John James was an affectionate as well as a caring parent, content to settle
quietly with his wife – who suffered from asthma – after their first years of
wandering. In September 1828, with 10 children living, they lost a baby son,
Daniel Finucane – called after Bidz's father, and baptised two days before he
died at the age of three weeks. So two years later, when she was expecting her
next child, Francis Nesbitt, Bidz stayed with her own family at Stamer Park,
in order to avoid the measles, which was afflicting the other children. She
took Georgina with her. A touching letter from John James tells her they are
now 'as well as possible', 'Johnny nearly well'. 'Janey', he said, 'My constant
bedfellow. . . . Jamsey just come in to give you a bag of kisses.' And he sent
'a thousand loves to you & dear Georgy'.

Carn Cross, his eldest son, was a sore disappointment to John James. He
was a young man in his 20s when Kitzy was a child, had been educated at a
public school in England, and found a good situation in the Navy Pay Office
in London. But he fell into bad company – Kate mentions two Dicksons,
brothers of Aunt Hessie, Uncle Henry of Rockwood's wife – and was drawn
into a life of dissipation. In his letter of March 1830 to Bidz, while she was

---

10. The fish was slashed, or 'crimped', before rigor mortis set in, in order to firm the flesh.

expecting Francis at Ennis, the first hint of trouble is introduced. John James asked Bidz if she could use her influence on her uncle Giles (now retired to Stamer Park from Dublin) to 'work some interest in London' for Carn Cross. 'It would be a sad business to have the poor fellow put down in the office now. There is not a moment to be lost.'

However, Carn Cross lost his position, and came home to Skreeney in disgrace. Kate, in her one criticism of her father, suggested that, if he had treated his son with more compassion, he might have turned out better. But her father never spoke to Carn Cross, and only allowed him to live in the house on sufferance, with the result that he spent his time in the village in low company, and never made a career for himself.[11]

Neither would Johnny Marcus, the third son, 14 years old when his youngest sister was born. He was to settle at Manorhamilton, where he held the post of Barony Constable, until he was duped by an associate – who absconded with the County Cess[12] – and was dismissed. He found temporary employment as a rate collector, until he emigrated to America, and became a book keeper in an iron foundry. Giles William, the brother in-between Carn Cross and John Marcus, and of a more solid temperament than either, was brought up at Ennis by Grandmother Finucane, Uncle Michael, and Great Uncle Giles in the expectation of inheriting the estate.

Her older sisters would become close friends of Kate later in life. They were educated at home by various governesses, one of whom was sent away by her father – though a great favourite with her pupils – 'for being too well versed in the art of mild flirtation, of which my father did not see the advantage.' Kate met one of the governesses, some years after Bessie and Diana had married, a 'Mrs' or 'Granny' Galbraith.

> On beginning her life as a governess, she called herself Mrs Galbraith' (tho' never married), as being more dignified; but, on being taken to task by my sister Diana for assuming brevet rank, she immediately saw her error, dropped the title and was 'Miss R. Galbraith' ever after.

Granny Galbraith was unusually plain and tiny, with protruding teeth, and Jemmy made a caricature sketch of her making toast, and giving directions at the same time about her tea to Miss Jane, and about the making of her cap to Diana, then Mrs Faris:

> Toast to-night, Miss Jane, and white sugar. But a small portion of the latter. Now, Mrs Faris, with regard to the cap. I'm to have a satin horseshoe up the back, and I have the greatest hatred to have my ribbon cut.

---

11. After John James died, Bidz had to support Carn Cross, and he died comparatively young, at the Whitworth Hospital in Dublin, in 1860.
12. The assessment (tax or levy).

In the sketch, Jemmy showed how the soles of her shoes had been built up to increase her height.

In winter, Kate recalled, Granny Galbraith wore a crimson cashmere dress, and in summer a muslin with green stripes, and she had a chain 'like a jack chain with large links' attached to her eye-glass, which the family said contained a piece of common glass.

Possibly the first big event in Kate's life was the marriage of her sister Bessie, who was 21 in March 1836, when Kate was only three. Bessie – handsome, amusing and vivacious – made a good match, choosing Noblett St Leger (pronounced 'Sellenger'), a civil engineer, who was County Surveyor in Leitrim at the time, and one of the St Legers of Heywards Hill in Cork. Shortly afterwards they moved to Sligo, where St Leger made many changes, designing both of the new bridges, and planning the approach of the railway line to the town. He was a reliable, congenial man, respected and liked by John James, who corresponded with him: and Bessie – or Bessy – supplied the girls back at Skreeney with the necessary trimmings for the Sligo Ball or the races, sent down by box in the post-car.[13]

Diana, as lovely as Bessy, but more susceptible, married just a year later at the age of 17. Her groom was a man who played a great part in the Cullen affairs, Alick Faris, Clerk-of-the-Peace for Leitrim, who lived at Shannon Lodge, in Carrick-on-Shannon. He was a good deal older than Diana, 'his tastes totally dissimilar to hers in every way, he was a curious mixture of good nature, carelessness and Lawyer's trickery', according to Kate.

The family had reason to remember Diana's wedding with sorrow, because Bessie brought her baby to Skreeney for the festivities and, neglected by his nurse, he took cold and died the day after the wedding. Bessie never had another child.

Diana went to Dublin for her wedding trip, where a dinner party was held in her honour by Sarah Curran's brother. (Tom Moore's sister was there too.) William Henry Curran had been assistant barrister at Manorhamilton, and was friendly with the Cullen family, but Noblett St Leger's family had known the now legendary Sarah intimately, and it was while she was staying with them in Cork that Robert Emmet was taken prisoner and condemned to death. Kate writes:

> I have often heard the St Legers tell the story of how this devoted girl ate Emmet's letters which she possessed – not being able to get rid of them in any other way, and, being fearful, if found on her, their contents might incriminate Emmet.

Kate had her first lessons from Diana's sister-in-law, Sara Faris – a clever

---

13. John James Cullen to Noblett St Leger, September 12, 1836.

well-educated woman – while both were staying at Diana's new home, Shannon Lodge, just outside Carrick-on-Shannon in County Leitrim. Kate claimed she was taught to read in six weeks, and afterwards she learned the rudiments of English, as well as the Church Catechism and the Commandments, from Miss Faris, who was 'very well versed in politics, a high Conservative, a strong Protestant, and of very decided views.'

But during her first 10 years, living at Skreeney, the three younger boys, – Paddy, Jemmy, and especially Francis – were company for Kitzy, together with the youngest of her four sisters, Janey, eight years older than herself. Francis was her special playmate, since mollycoddled Jemmy had no interest in boyish games. Kate made herself 'as like a boy as possible' for Francis' sake.

Patrick Edmund, or Paddy, born in 1823, was in her opinion 'the flower of the flock',

> the handsomest, cleverest, wittiest, and possessing the warmest heart and the most affectionate disposition, along with the most charming manners, a favourite everywhere.

Paddy was educated at Portora Royal School, and took the highest prizes and certificates, according to his sister. When preparing for Trinity College, his father engaged a series of tutors, who taught not only Paddy and his younger brothers, but Kate as well, and two of the cousins from Rockwood. Kate remembered one tutor named Carmody, 'who had the audacity to flog me, for which he was threatened with a sound beating by my cousin, Paddy Cullen.' Kate must have been about eight at the time.

Carmody left, and was succeeded by the very popular Mr Willis, who taught Kitzy French. However he departed, declaring that he did not think it proper to go on teaching them when Paddy already knew more than he did. Mr Maguire, later Dean Maguire, who followed, was a good classical master. Kate's memory of the schoolroom was of him reading Homer and Virgil with Paddy and of Paddy's deep beautiful voice repeating his words.

3

Sunsweet Air

Skreeney, Donegal, Clare, Sligo, Leitrim, 1832-1842

Life passed in a leisurely way at Skreeney – a quiet country existence, patterned with visits from relations like the Farises, St Legers and Labatts, or Grandmother Finucane from Clare in the early days, or Aunt Stacpoole. The occasional stranger staying at the house would be taken for a drive into Sligo, over the mountainous road which terminated in a wide view of the Atlantic, with perhaps the sight of a four-master in full sail, setting out for Glasgow and Liverpool. The scenery was delightful, and Sligo was already famous for its mountains, waterfalls, and the beautiful Lough Gill, which would be a much nearer attraction for the outside world with the advent of the railway.

The older ladies often went to Sligo for a day's shopping, and brought back oranges and sweets to the expectant children, who had no such luxuries obtainable in Manorhamilton, and who descended eagerly on the orangeman's cart when it was seen coming up the avenue on one of its rare journeys from Sligo. The only sweets Kate remembered from her early years of the 1830s were sugar candy, barley sugar, peppermint rock and sugar stick.

> A great event at Skreeney was the arrival of an organ or hurdy-gurdy man, with perhaps a monkey, who would come on the long car from Enniskillen or Sligo. He would be brought in and given a good dinner, and sent on his way rejoicing. These visits were like angels' as there were of course no trains in those days.

There were many beggars and tramps about Skreeney in those days, as around other demesnes. As she wrote, looking back at the end of the century, Kate commented

> The costume of the old tramps and beggars was different to what it is now. The women generally wore thick white caps with borders, a black petticoat or a flannel one and a quilt round their shoulders, and carrying a child or perhaps two on their backs. Denis Ryan, a beggar, called 'Donald Blue', wore a quilt with tufts on it, fastened with a skewer, and wore nothing else . . . Donald Blue's head was cropped quite close.

> I heard a cousin of mine, Henry Palmer, tell how, driving near Dromahair one day there was a stone in the road, Donald was coming along and

Henry Palmer being in a hurry called out to him, 'Take that stone out of that, Denis.' Donald not doing as he was asked, Henry called again: 'Take that stone to hell out of that.' Denis on this removed the stone and turning to Henry said: 'When you go to that place, Denis Ryan won't be there to take the stone out of your road.'

Before dinner was over, the beggars were gathering at the back door of the big house for food and Kate used to avoid them. But she made friends with two beggar children, one a Maureen Fogherty, and the other a pretty girl called 'Miss Plunkett' – daughter of a miserable-looking woman with a sack about her shoulders. Kitzy would steal off down the avenue with her bread and jam to play with them and, if discovered by one of the tutors, was in disgrace.

One beggar who frequented the Boyle or Carrick area was called 'The Height of Honour' or 'Noble Blood'. 'Fair Queen' was another character, who had a romantic past. She was a Miss Kirkwood who had run away with a lover who had deserted her and she had gone astray in her mind.

Her peculiarity was wearing three or four bonnets one on top of the other. . . . We were always looking out for her numerous bonnets when in Church. She generally sat on one of the steps going up to the gallery, and when I was waiting for my mother to come out from the Sacrament I used to be afraid of 'Fair Queen' and shut myself into the vestry, or go into Blair the Sexton's to avoid her.

Within Skreeney's large household, Kate as a child had her own maid, a pious Methodist named Jane Duncan, daughter of an army farrier, with whom she had tussles at night when it came to applying the curling papers.

Of the people who lived about the house and place, I remember Rorke the gardener, who was married to a girl of the name of Crowle, daughter of our housemaid, Kitty. Kitty Crowle was a daughter of 'Mary the Laundry', a handsome old woman wearing her hair in a French tête, a splendid laundress, with a very good tongue. . . .

The Steward was Bob Wilson, a stout little man with very fat legs, who had a habit of frightening me out of the yard by shaking the skirts of his coat at me. He was husband to Peggy Wilson, a former nursery maid. Jimmy O'Brien and his daughters . . . lived in a comfortable cottage about a quarter of a mile off.

Since tea and sugar were precious commodities in those days the servants at Skreeney were given dry tea from the breakfast table each morning, with sugar in an egg cup. Mary the Laundry and Jane Duncan alone were treated differently, and received their tea in a bowl.

that however as I have always considered her an ideal laundress.
The Steward was Bob Wilson a stout little man with very fat legs,
who had a habit of frightening me out of the yard by shaking the
skirts of his coat at me, which had the effect of terrifying me -
why I don't know. He was husband to Peggy Wilson a former
nursery maid. Jimmy O'Brien and his daughters, Susanna &
lived in a comfortable cottage about a quarter of a mile off. We
often enjoyed a good tea with them but unhappily Susanna took it
into her head to go to America, after which the tea ceased. She
returned however and supported her father in his old age.

          Talking of tea, which was a precious commodity in those
days as well as sugar, the servants at Skreeney got dry tea (in a
saucer and sugar in an egg cup) from the breakfast table each morning, but "Mary the Laundry" got hers in a bowl. Jane Duncan my
maid got hers in a bowl also. The servants all spoke Irish among
themselves, everyone in the kitchen spoke it, and I have been told
that my father who was foster-nursed by the Feeney's came home
speaking Irish and spoke nothing else till he was 7 years old. My
Uncle Stacpoole in the Co. Clare also spoke Irish well and trans-
acted his business with his tenants in that language, I wish to
state here that Irish has only been lost for one generation, that
is my own, I am ashamed to say, and not wholly lost, being familiar
to me in the nursery and kitchen though only partially understood,
I hear a great deal about its revival at the present day but it
was never a dead language to me, and both in Leitrim and Donegal
was spoken all round me in my childhood. A foster sister of my

                                                        father's

Typed page of memoir. Private collection, Dublin.

All the servants spoke Irish among themselves. Kate was familiar with it
from the nursery, and it was the common language in the kitchen. Her father
had been foster-nursed in a local family, and when he came home spoke
nothing else until he was seven years old; and Uncle Stacpoole in Clare also
spoke Irish, and conducted business with his tenants in the native tongue.

Gorman had come to Skreeney from the Leitrim Militia when it was disbanded. He was an excellent butler, 'usually wore a plain black 'bodycoat', waistcoat and trousers and white tie; but on state occasions he wore a coat of the Cullen livery – blue cloth with white pocket – flaps fastened down, with livery buttons crested.' He frequently beat his wife – the first trained nurse from Dublin's Rotunda maternity hospital to practise in Leitrim – when he wanted money for drink, using his trusty blackthorn, named by him 'Faithful'!

Gorman was also a flute-player, and played at all the Skreeney dances. Kate remembered her father leading off at a country dance in the hall at Christmas time, wearing an ordinary dress suit, and perhaps a waistcoat 'embroidered with gold (or of blue tabinet[1]) appearing a little above the ordinary waistcoat (which was sometimes of cut black velvet, spotted with gold) which was a fashion at that time.'

One of her sister Bessie's friends, Anne Tottenham of the Tottenhams of Glenfarne, was a constant visitor. She was very pretty, but because of her father's extravagance had little to spend on clothes.

> I have often heard Bessie tell of her arrival at Skreeney for a Christmas party: how she would arrive up on a car with her young brother, carrying a carpet-bag containing her dress – a plain white muslin one – rolled up in a 'wisp'.

(The fashion during Bessie's girlhood for straight muslin dresses must have been a godsend for young ladies living in the country, with miles to travel to a friend's house, or to the nearest town, for a ball.)

> This (which had been worn several times already) she would shake out, and, on her hair being done by some of our girls, would put on; and afterwards would look prettier and more stylish than anyone in the room.

The young people danced to the music of a harpsichord, played by Great Aunt Manly. It still stood in the hall as Kitzy grew up, a handsome piece of furniture, but it was impossible to have it tuned.

Kitzy herself paid lengthy visits to her three married sisters in Donegal, Sligo and Carrick-on-Shannon. In Donegal, while her mother and the other children went to Clare, she was allowed to run wild and came back, not only unmanageable, but without her curls, to the great disgust of her father. Mary Labatt had found the curling too much trouble.

---

1.   Tabinet, which was much used in Ireland about this period, was a watered fabric made from silk and wool to resemble poplin.

The Labatt's Rectory was a fine house some distance away from Mount Charles village, set in woods looking straight down reedy fields to the sea, and a view of low hills. It was built of random stone, with a single dormer window over the front door. At the time there was no church nearer than Inver. The Labatts spent some time at Lord Mount Charles's shooting lodge a mile away, when the family were in residence in the summer. Edward taught Kitzy to ride, and took her out on the water, sometimes under cliffs, which rise 1,900 feet above sea level. The coast guards watched out for him on stormy days, because he could be reckless, but Kate regretted that they never succeeded in getting into the caves, which could only be approached on a fair day at low tide, when the wind was in the right direction.

In County Clare, at Ballyalla, lived Aunt Stacpoole – sister of Kitzy's mother – the third wife of Andrew Stacpoole, tall and good-looking, with a pleasant manner, though her complexion, in the opinion of the family, was too red. The Cullens posted down to Clare by carriage, changing horses at the various places where they put up for the night by the way. One stop was at Edenvale, where Uncle Stacpoole's eldest daughter by a previous wife was married to Richard Stacpoole. On a ridge above the Kilrush road, the house was approached through marshy meadowland. Below the ivy-clad rock on which the bleak Georgian building stands are caves, and a stepped walk leads to a secluded lake. The gaunt, melancholy house might have been conjured up by Emily Brontë.

Kate's grandmother's house, Stamer Park, in Ennis – another stop – was now the seat of Uncle Michael Finucane, and was homely by contrast. It was a modest two-storey house, set in its own grounds, a walled garden dividing it from the dignified remains of Ennis Friary. The Friary was regarded as an attraction by contemporaries for its 'grand eastern window',[2] its abbot's chair, and the altar with figures carved in relief.

Later, when Kitzy's cousin, Kate Stacpoole, married Austin Butler of Ballyline, Kitzy and her mother might stay at Ballyline on the way, but the joy of their journey to Clare was the arrival at Ballyalla. To Kate Cullen it seemed that the sun always shone at Ballyalla. It was a pretty house, surrounded by woods and beech trees, raised on a hill above a lake three miles from Ennis. The house, she tells in her memoir, had been built by her uncle and had all the modern improvements.[3]

> In the garden grew Grapes, Nectarines and Peaches, Plums, etc., a great attraction to us youngsters. . . . Beside the house was a lovely hill where we played as children. That hill was the dream of my childhood. It was covered with wild strawberries, which we used to gather on what the

---

2.   S. Lewis, *A Topographical Dictionary of Ireland*. Vol. L, 1837, p. 602.
3.   It has been greatly altered since then.

Stamer Park, Ennis. (Author's photograph.)

country people called 'taneens'. There was a young plantation of firs, larches and other trees, and a path through it which led to the top.

My cousin Kitty (Kate Stacpoole) was always working with silk worms and she used to go up there to gather mulberry leaves for them. I liked it because the sun seemed to be always shining there, and there were lovely blue butterflies with drab underneath, and speckled, and dragon flies, and many other delightful things of that kind, and Kate Stacpoole was very learned on these subjects and knew all about insects, and when the strawberries ought to appear.

Kate is harsh about her cousin Kitty's two brothers, Willie and Andrew, and their 'Clare vulgarity'. Aunt Stacpoole attempted to correct this by moving to Cheltenham when Uncle Stacpoole died, to improve their education. She succeeded – Kate remarks – 'in making fine blackguards' of them. 'Not that she intended to do so'! Willie eventually went into Parliament as Member for Ennis, despite the scathing criticism of his sister who said, 'Isn't it enough for you to be making a fool of yourself at home, without going into Parliament to do it?' Whatever pretensions they may have had to refinement, the family, like the Cullens and other landed Protestants, retained a sturdy bluntness of speech.

Days were free and easy at Ballyalla, the breakfast late, the company drifting downstairs at any time.

> The Carriage was ordered after the late breakfast, and my Aunt drove into Ennis every day accompanied by her guests. She always went in to see her Aunt Dowling. She was a very handsome old lady, always very well dressed, and took a peculiar pleasure in slipping gifts into the hands of children, who always liked to go and see her. She generally wore a brown tabinet or brown corded silk and a lace cap. . . .

> There were two other old ladies on the Causeway as it was called, Nancy Power and Mary Creagh, also Dr and Mrs O'Brien, an old couple, and their daughter, Mary Jane . . . whom my Aunt also generally visited. She would be back in time for 6 o'c dinner, and I remember that she always brought back sweets from town, 'bulls' eyes', which all Clare youngsters delighted in.

> One peculiarity about the Stacpoole dinner was that, no matter what the other dishes were, a beef steak always appeared with it. This would be brought round to my Uncle Stacpoole, and perhaps a piece the size of a half a crown only would be taken out of it, but it had to be there. Willie afterwards always strictly adhered to this religious rite.

> After this dinner came on the yard dinner, which was dealt round by the kitchen maid to all the beggars who had congregated by this time in the yard and produced their cans ready for carriage home of bacon, or corned mutton and cabbage. A side of bacon was put down every day for this purpose, and cut up by Kitty the cook.

Kitzy often saw the beggars crowding round the kitchen door, with a piper or two playing at the hall door, and this custom continued in Willie's time also, after Uncle Stacpoole had passed on.
'They had beautiful cows at Ballyalla,' she recalls,

> and my Uncle S. always sat on a seat under the parlour window to see them passing to be milked every evening. Everyday after dinner, Harry Connolly the butcher came out from Ennis to impart to my Uncle Stacpoole such pleasing intelligence as the state of the market, the price of wool, cattle etc.

> He would sit in the parlour after we had all gone out to play, to swing in the shrubbery, or to ride on my Uncle's quiet old pony, while my Uncle mixed for himself and Harry the fragrant tumblers of punch, to which no one could give the flavour as well as he.

> After this my Uncle would sit in the drawing-room and have his hair

combed by Lucy Brew, or Mary Jane O'Brien. He had a fine head of hair for an elderly man, and no doubt enjoyed the ministrations of the two young ladies. He has sometimes fallen asleep under the process. Another curious habit of his was always getting his new clothes broken in by John Butler, the Steward, who wore them first, making them easier for the wearer.

Uncle Stacpoole's brother was Dean of Kilfenora but Uncle Andrew's family, except for his wife Diana, were of an irreligious turn. As a child, Kitzy found life in Clare quite a contrast to her own home, where the days always began with the reading of scriptures, and family prayer and she comments that her father – with his disciplined nature – never liked to prolong his visits to Ballyalla, and did not care for Clare people in general. This attitude explains in part her own mixed views about the Stacpoole family, much as she enjoyed the summer visits there.

> When Uncle Andrew was dying, the Dean tried to direct his thoughts towards the world beyond, and spoke of the glories of Heaven, but was interrupted by Andrew saying, 'Ballyalla's good enough for me – if I was left in it.'

One of the delights of Ballyalla for Kate, who was musical, was that Aunt Stacpoole would bring professional singers to the house from the capital. Kate had a sweet voice, and learned much from them. She remembered the celebrated Mrs Waylett, who had a magnificent voice, much admired in Dublin, and Uncle Michael Finucane bringing other Dublin singers in his coach to Stamer Park for the enjoyment of the local gentry.

Kate first visited the St Legers in Sligo on a day trip from Skreeney, when her mother went for a day's shopping. Later she was allowed to go alone to stay with Bessie and Noblett at the house they then occupied in Quay Street. Subsequently they lived in Wine Street, and they finally moved to a grander house on the Mall, with steps up to a front porch, which had doors on either side. Kitzy walked with a servant, Pat Fannin, to Sligo Quay to look at the masted ships. Pat wore his livery coat.

> I used to feel greatly insulted when the children of the poorer class would shout after us: 'Oh! look at the man-maid!'

She liked to stay with Bessie, who was immensely hospitable and had a keen sense of fun, overlooking what the other relatives 'deemed grievous faults. She always said that it was a libel on me to say that I was a bold child, as she thought I was very good.' Noble St Leger [Sellenger] often took her with him when he was going to Mrs Wilson's to look for the latest periodicals and books. Kate was to see here, for the first time in Sligo, what were known

Page of manuscript memoir. Private collection, Dublin.

as the 'Green Books' – a series entitled *The Parlour Library* – which introduced her to Jane Austen's novels, and the stories of Mrs Gaskell.

Kitzy also had happy memories of her sister Diana's house, Shannon Lodge, in County Leitrim. Shannon Lodge no longer exists. It was a characterful house standing on the far side of the bridge outside Carrick-on-Shannon, in its own demesne. The castellation over the central portcullis entrance contrasted with the rural-style gables, rising above the side windows. Farises had lived there for a century.

The beautiful Diana gathered admirers round her, one of whom was Bennett Little, whom Kate knew as boy and man, and who became agent to Lt-Colonel Edward King Tennison. Kate enjoyed the humour and bonhomie of the Little family. Bennett, his brother Roper and their witty mother lived at the King Tennison dower house at Knockranny, and she spent many a pleasant day there. They were well-read eccentrics.

> When staying at Knockranny you were sometimes rather startled by seeing the butler entering the dining room late at night, and laying the cloth, and a pretty substantial breakfast appearing immediately after. To your expression of astonishment at this, the butler would reply, 'Did you not know, Sir (or Miss), that the Master always takes his breakfast the night before he goes to a Fair? Tomorrow is the Fair of Boyle, and he wants to lose no time in the morning.'

None of the members of Parliament for Leitrim or Sligo at the time was greatly distinguished, according to Kate, though she had an affection for Edward King Tenison, who got her brother Francis into the Constabulary. She was also impressed that Colonel Tenison's wife, Lady Louisa, an artist, took a prominent part in politics. She recalled the uneasiness that prevailed at election time while she was staying at Shannon Lodge.

> I remember at one of these elections, troops were stationed in Carrick, and, being on duty all day in the street, the people handed out loaves of bread to them through the windows. One night an alarm was given that a riot had broken out in Mohill, and the soldiers were ordered off there. The whole town gathered to see them start and there was great excitement, but, when they arrived in Mohill, they found that the only disturbance was the catching of a flock of geese, that had been startled; the inhabitants were quietly asleep in their beds, and the soldiers had their ten miles' ride for nothing.

> It was during this election or another that the order was given by Lord Leitrim, who was Custos Rotulorum[4] of the county then, that every man's blackthorn should be seized as he entered the town, as a riot was expected (blackthorns being the favourite weapon of the Leitrim men). The blackthorns were accordingly seized at the bridge, and they were handed over to the charge of Mr (Alick) Faris [Diana's husband], who then was Clerk of the Peace; and were conveyed to Shannon Lodge, where there was a great collection of them for some time. But as every visitor who wished for a blackthorn was free to take one, in time they all disappeared.

---

4.   Chief Justice of the Peace

Kate writes of another remarkable personality in Leitrim, 'Mrs Mac', or 'the Widow Peyton' of Laheen, a strict Catholic. Originally a Miss Reynolds, she liked to remember that the Reynoldses came of the Clan Mac Ranalt. She and her sister, Biddy Reynolds, used to spend much time at Kilmore House, the residence of the Bishop, and were involved in local charities.

Biddy Reynolds, was as handsome as 'Mrs Mac' was ugly. Kate says that she was fond of practical jokes, 'not always of a refined nature: some of them I dare not mention in these respectable memoirs'. However, she tells one story, and many another must have circulated in the Cullen family.

> It related to a shy curate, and occurred at Kilmore. One afternoon when she and this curate were alone in the drawing-room, everyone else being out, she told him she was going to teach him a new game. First he must lock the door, and put the key in his pocket.
>
> This having been done, she told him to cross his hands. Taking his handkerchief she tied them together; then, telling him to raise his arms, she dexterously slipped in her head under them and then began to shout at the top of her voice for help. The servants came to the door and tried to open it, and she called out, 'He's locked it, he's got the key in his pocket.'
>
> When at last they got in through the window, and freed Biddy, the wretched curate jumped out of the window, took to his heels, and was never seen again in that neighbourhood.'

'Mrs Mac' could be as peremptory in her treatment of others as Biddy was. She had two granddaughters, who used to visit Shannon Lodge.

> Mary Anne was very pretty with very refined features, very good mouth and teeth, nez retroussé, and pretty grey eyes, her hair fair and her manner most taking. She was very clever, her grandmother's wit, which was very keen, coming out in all she said and did. She played and sang very well. She was a great friend of mine, and we had very pleasant days together.
>
> Of course, she was considered rather fast in those slow days, but she was so fascinating and pretty, that she was forgiven much. Her sister Eliza tried to imitate her, but could not succeed in being like her, as she was not at all so pretty, though I have sometimes seen her look very well.
>
> Once when they were staying at Shannon Lodge, and had been to a ball at Boyle, their Granny desired them to be home on a certain day. Not heeding this, they did not come home till the next night, and their Granny was so mad with them that she would not let them into the house, and they had to sleep in the carriage all night!

One of Kate's last memories of childhood in County Leitrim was of the introduction of the penny post, in 1840. Before that, the Cullen family used to ask any Member of Parliament who might be staying at Skreeney to frank their letters. He would sign his name in the corner of the folded letter, or on the letter paper, which, when the letter was written, was folded up, and sealed at the back with wax. Otherwise, Kitzy's father would send a bundle of letters over with a servant to the Member for Leitrim at that time, Tom White, and ask him to frank them.

Kate remembered the day the penny post came into being. With Jemmy and Francis, all armed with pens and paper, she sat down and wrote a letter to the Stacpooles in Clare. All began their letter the same way, 'I take advantage of the penny post to address a letter to you, expecting to receive one from you in return.'

4

And so I Came to Dublin

Dublin 1840s

John James Cullen died in 1842. He was only 59. No cause for his death is given, but Uncle Henry Cullen, who had recently moved to Carrick-on-Shannon as Secretary to the Grand Jury of Leitrim, died two months before him of the common plague of those times, typhus fever.

For Kate it meant not only the uprooting of her immediate family, because Skreeney still belonged to Carney Cullen, but a shadow was cast over their financial affairs, and relations with the Faris in-laws became strained.

Kate, barely 10, saw Alick and John Faris descend on Skreeney, and drink all the choice wine in the cellar – 'supplied by Wisdom the Wine Merchant, very precious'. If Alick Faris's true character now revealed itself to her – too young to have been fully aware of his deviousness before this – she was also conscious of how Edward Labatt, who had never measured up to her father's expectations, stood by Bidz and the children, and managed to save some of the furniture (including the 'modern' mahogany bed) from the agents, to pack it on the cart for going to Dublin.

Kate draws a veil over the events she learned of gradually from her bruised mother during the years that followed. She never knew the complete details, but the family were quite certain that they had been duped by the Faris brothers.

> 'I have always smarted under the statement which was dinned into my infant ears, that my dear Father died in debt and did not leave enough to pay off his liabilities. It was perfectly untrue, the rents of 3 large farms were received and the money paid into the Courts for several years by the two Agents. The debts were not paid, and no accounts given to anyone of the money ... the whole business, 'Cullen's Minors', was for years the laughing stock of the Dublin Four Courts.

Kate blamed John Faris chiefly. Alick, her sister Diana's husband, she considered was not bad by nature, but was indolent, and let John do what he wished. Alick was kindly and hospitable, and his house was open to any members of the family who chose to stay there. He was particularly kind to Kitzy, and, when – capping the unfortunate happenings at Skreeney – John Marcus found himself in trouble and lost his position in Manorhamilton as

Barony Constable, Alick Faris brought him to Shannon Lodge, where he lived for some years, and got some temporary employment under the Poor Law Board as a Rate Collector.

Nevertheless, Alick Faris lost nothing by such kindnesses. He and a Doctor Tait of Manorhamilton acted as sureties for John Marcus.

> Alick Faris paid it all then, but he amply repaid himself afterwards in two or three ways. One act was making my mother give up all the family plate to him, for the purpose, he said, of paying debts of my father's. He kept the plate for himself, sold his own plate and also the large Salver presented to my father by the Militia.

Clearly there was rage and indignation among the Cullens. John Marcus, whose large attractive hand contrasts with the precision of his father's flowing script, listed over 50 items of silver, which they subsequently forfeited, in an inventory made on November 21, 1842. The list included asparagus tongs, one Tea Digester, one Ring (presumably a dish ring, which is peculiar to Irish silver, and used for holding potatoes or hot dishes),[1] 8 Wine Coasters, one Snuff dish, and numerous spoons and forks for various purposes. The stylish life of Skreeney had come to an abrupt end.

By the terms of their father's life insurance, the three eldest daughters, Mary Labatt, Bessie St Leger and Diana Faris, each received £1000. Bidz's fortune of £3000, given to her by her uncle Giles Daxon on her marriage, had purchased a small property, Tully and Largey, and this had been settled on her and her children, and would be her means of support. She moved to Dublin with the six who remained under her care, and took a house in Percy Place.

The talented Paddy had been at Trinity College for a year, studying for an Arts Degree. John James had intended him for the Bar but, perhaps shocked at his father's death and aware of his mother's straitened circumstances, or, alternatively, free now to do as he himself wished, he left college, and set about plans to make a career for himself in India.

Two undated letters to his sisters survive which indicate him to be as attractive and fun-loving as he had been as a teenager – one is to Georgy (Georgina), the other to Jane. He was staying with their elder brother, Giles, who had been brought up by Grandmother Finucane at Stamer Park, but who now lived at New Ross, in Wexford.

Giles had been led to understand that he would be Uncle Michael's heir and had never trained for any profession. Life at Stamer Park had been a succession of horses and dogs, and outdoor pastimes until

one fine day his Uncle took unto himself a wife. This wife was an only

---

1. In John James Cullen's shorter list of 1822, this is noted as weighing 16½ oz.

child, and had a lot of money, and, as Uncle Michael had been rather extravagant, he wanted the money. His wife was the only child of Pierce Carrick, an Attorney, and Land Agent, who was shot sometime in the early 'Forties' – that time so fatal to Landlords and Agents.

(Giles – denied of his expected inheritance – showed his mettle, and obtained an appointment in the Revenue Police, known at the time as the 'Poteen Hussars'. After a few years, he moved to the Royal Irish Constabulary).[2]

He was in Rosbercon, New Ross, having recently moved from Thomastown in County Kilkenny, when Paddy stayed with him. Rosbercon was, Patrick told Janey:

> Giles's long wished-for station. He applied for it himself and succeeded. But alas! the great attraction is gone (namely the widow), she has left this to the great grief of her numerous friends and acquaintances. But I am not so lonely as Giles. Four very nice girls, the Miss Fishers, sing and play delightfully. I am just now come from paying them a visit. I dined only one day at home since we came to these parts, that looks well, eh, old girl?

Janey was staying with the St Legers when he wrote, and Paddy wanted to know if there was 'any fun in the dancing line going on in Sligo'.

He and Giles were trying to persuade their mother to leave Dublin and make her home in Rosbercon, the house being much bigger than that in Percy Place. It would be very cheap. Bidz was worried about Jemmy and the guardianship, but Paddy did not see any problem 'as she could take a run up to town occasionally for the large sum of 5-6'.

Paddy's second letter, this time to Georgy, reiterates the invitation to Mamma to come and reside in New Ross, and also begs Georgy to send 'as soon as possible the words and Music of 'I would I were a Fairy' – as I promised to get them for a pretty girl who lives near this.' He and Georgy evidently made a practice of teasing one another, because he went on –

> Send them when you receive this like a good girl. Your hair is not at all red indeed it is not now

– and added that it was great fun where they were in Rosbercon, they could be out every night.

Jemmy, the particular pet of his mother, had been educated at home, and entered Trinity College at the age of 20 in 1846 as a pensioner, intended by

---

2.   The story had an ironical ending to it, since eighty years later, after Kate's death, Michael's sole descendant died childless, and Susan Mitchell – Giles's niece and one of the beneficiaries of her cousin Pierce Finucane's estate – was able to invest in a house.

his mother for the Church. Aunt Stacpoole was paying for him. If they went away, Bidz worried continually about his being back in Dublin for his studies, 'which', Kate remarks dryly, 'I never could see came to anything.' The College Calender lists him as a Senior Freshman in 1847 but he does not appear in its pages for 1848. Janey and Georgy used to visit Sligo and Carrick-on-Shannon – Francis had been adopted by the Farises and lived at Carrick but, apart from some hurried trip to Clare, Jemmy and Kate would spend most of their time in Dublin.

Gorman had accompanied the depleted family to Dublin, and used to bring Kate to school each morning,

> used to call for me at school every day and carry home my basket of books. He also used to bring me home from parties and scold me well for keeping him waiting in the hall, greatly to the amusement of my girl friends, one of whom used to come downstairs to see me off and to hear the scolding!

Kate left an account of her education in Dublin during the early 1840s. The school was run by a Miss Gregg, who had been governess to Noblett St Leger's sister at one time.

> The school was at 36, Lower Mount Street, and there I learned English, French and Music from Masters – John Moses taught music, piano, theory, etc. English was taught by Mr Lloyd and by Miss Gregg herself, who also taught music very well, and taught Grecian, Roman and English History, writing etc. Having a good voice, my Mother had me taught singing by Mr Toole, who was one of the choristers of St Patrick's [Cathedral] and organist of St Mary's (Rutland Square). He was an excellent teacher. After I left school, I had finishing lessons from Dr Francis Robinson one of the first teachers in Dublin.

> I also learned dancing at the school from Mr Williams, and Monsieur Barnet, who both taught one day each every week. . . . We learned waltzing, and then came into fashion the polka (which was learned by everyone who learned dancing), quadrilles and the lancers.

> Miss Gregg gave a party every Christmas, at which these dances were shown off. Mr Williams and Mons. Barnet were invited, and the brothers, parents and friends of the pupils all came. The girls wore white frocks, clear muslin with tucks, and sometimes black velvet bodies with them. I am told I was a very pretty child, notwithstanding the depredations of my sister, Mary Labatt, my hair was long and thick: it was plaited and turned up, which was the fashion. These parties we enjoyed very much.

Kate remained friendly with Miss Gregg long after she had left the school, and thought her 'a very charming little woman, with very good manners'. She had bright brown eyes, and black hair, which she wore in ringlets in front, and turned up at the back, with combs keeping the curls in their place in front – the current fashion. Miss Gregg was the talented member of her family, and was fluent in French, Italian and German, after travelling abroad as governess to Dean Blacker of Mullabrack's daughters in her youth.

Miss Fanny Gregg was as modern in her hair style as her sister. She had blue eyes, and was rather pretty, but the girls did not care so much for her as for Miss Gregg. Kate preferred another sister, a Mrs Robinson, who ran a small school of her own in Percy Place.

Kate's friends at school included Amelia O'Connor, daughter of one of the actresses at Fishamble Street, who had been adopted by a Mrs Davis – sister of the writer, Mrs Hemans – and who boarded at the school. Kate was sometimes asked to spend a few days at the school to keep Amelia company. Henrietta Bolton, whose father was an attorney, used to ask Kate back to her house in Lower Mount Street.

Another boarder and great friend was Henrietta Cornwall. Her father, who lived at Rutland Square, was agent to Lord Conyngham, and the family lived during the summer near the Labatts at Mount Charles in Donegal. Henrietta was very pretty, with blue eyes, fair hair turned up at the back, and her gold ringlets secured at the front with side combs; she had a beaver bonnet for outside wear. Her three brothers always came to Miss Gregg's parties, where Kate remembered dancing with them. In later life her picture was of the beaver bonnet, and of meeting the golden-haired Henrietta in town, arms linked with two of the brothers who were particularly fond of her.

Two other boarders were cousins – Henrietta and Agnes McNally.

> Agnes was born in India, and was sent home to Ireland to be educated at Miss Gregg's along with her cousin. Her Indian nurse had tied a piece of lead on her nose when she was a baby, as was the Indian custom. And, as this was done repeatedly, she had a flat spot on the top of her nose, which gave her a very foreign appearance. Her eyes were dark and had a very dreamy expression, and her hair (also dark) was in thick curls. She wore bright crimson and light green cashmere frocks and one would at once single her out as being foreign.

The Pyms, who were Quakers, were industrious. Mary Jane Whitsitt, on the other hand, got bad marks for her conduct every day and Mary Waddell was 'an idler who never learned anything'.

> There was a curious custom observed at the school which was that, when the judgements were reckoned up at the end of the month, the girl who had the most bad judgements was condemned to wear, pinned

on her breast, a piece of brown canvas, worked in red wool, with the following inscription: – *I am the young lady who had the most bad judgements last month.*

This she had to wear for the whole of the ensuing month, before the masters and all the girls. Mary Jane Whitsitt usually wore the badge, but was so accustomed to it that she never seemed to mind.

Miss Gregg provided amusement as well as work for her pupils. Her aunt, Mrs Finaigle – widow of one of the pioneer educationalists – was matron of the Rotunda Hospital, and lived on the premises, so there were always tickets for any entertainments held in the Rotunda Gardens.

There was a lake in the garden and various amusements went on within the grounds and in the Rotunda building, in the latter concerts, and in the gardens 'transparencies', which were very pretty, and were the same kind as those given in the Portobello Gardens. I remember seeing the latter: 'Herculaneum and Pompei', Florence with the Arno, Vesuvius and Etna, also 'Venice' with the gondolas on the water all about the bridge. The effect was produced by coloured lights thrown on artificial buildings, and was extremely good.

Miss Gregg often gave us this treat, and the great thing was marching two and two from Mount St to the Rotunda, where, after the entertainment, we would have tea with Mrs Finaigle, and then return to Miss Gregg's where we would wind up the evening with a dance.

Julian was a celebrated band conductor during Kitzy's youth, though she

The Rotunda New Rooms, Parnell Square, Dublin (detail), c.1820, artist unknown.
(Photograph courtesy of the National Gallery of Ireland no. 18,074.)

records the occasion when she heard him after her marriage. It was in the Rotunda Gardens.

> His band played the Post Horn Gallop, one man concealed in a tree playing the horn, and the band answering back. Julian's return was hailed with delight as he had not come over for many years, owing to a circumstance which had occurred during his last visit, when he gave a concert in the Music Hall, Abbey Street. He had with him the great Polish singer Pischek, who on singing 'The Standard Bearer' was violently encored. Rage seized Julian, as he had to pay 20 guineas for every encore, and he would not allow Pischek to sing again.

> Then began the grand row, shouting and booing: bad eggs, cold potatoes were procured by the crowd, and shied pell-mell, one landing on Julian's elaborate shirt-front. This was received by Julian with the words, 'What can you expect from an Irish mob'. This finished Julian's career in Dublin for many years; and the first time he dared to show his nose again was in the Rotunda Gardens.

After she left the Misses Gregg, Kate had a governess for a while, who was worthless, and that was the end of her schooling. However, she did continue to study music, keeping up singing lessons with Mr Toole, and then later going to Dr Francis Robinson to be 'finished'.

The Cullens' physican in Dublin was the son of an Ennis doctor, one of the 'Clare set' with whom Bidz associated, 'which included the O'Loughlens, ourselves and a few others' – all his patients.

> John Banks had been sent to Dublin by my Aunt Dowling to study for the medical profession. Being a young man of great promise and of pleasing manners he was well calculated to become successful, and she was able to help him in a pecuniary manner. He afterwards reached a high place in his profession, obtained a K.C.B.[4], and had a large practice.

> I remember once when I had measles in Percy Place and was rather bad, how he came in to see me in his castle dress, and sat watching me with his watch throughout the greater part of the night, till he could pronounce me out of danger. He was always a great friend of my mother's and of all the family. He used to clap me on the back when a child, and call me 'Kitzy, my fine fellow'.

During the summer after they gave up their first Dublin house in Percy Place, a friend, Mrs Kean, lent them her house in Lower Baggot Street while

---

3.   Knight Commander of the Order of the Bath.

she was away. There their aging butler Gorman created further scandal, persuading Julia the maid to marry him – unknown to the Cullens – even though his first wife was still living in Manorhamilton! 'A letter addressed to Julia as "Mrs Gorman" unveiled the secret', comments Kate.

No mention is made in the memoir of how the family sorted out such a complication, but the skittish Gorman was to settle down eventually with his daughter in Carrick-on-Shannon. His daughter, called Catherine after Kate, was nicknamed by the family 'The Heiress', because Gorman's sister was said to be 'intending' to leave Catherine the wealth she had accrued during her days as a huckster.

5

The Feast of Youth

Dublin 1840s

Dublin, at the time Kate arrived there, was leisurely and cultured; suffering from financial deprivation, due to political discrimination since the Union of 1800, but independently buoyant nevertheless. A Mrs Mitchell of Belfast, who published a commentary on her travels about Italy and the British Isles about 1840, described Leinster House, where the Royal Dublin Society had its museum, as 'the finest edifice' in the city. But

> the want of such a room as has been erected at the public expense for the exhibition of their minerals in the British Museum, made it expedient to arrange the specimens in lofty vertical, instead of horizontal cases; consequently those on the higher shelves cannot be viewed without great inconvenience.[1]

She denounced the successive British governments for gradually reducing grants to the Dublin Society, which played such a major part in the improvement of agriculture, arts and manufactures in Ireland, while enormous grants were consistently made to the British Museum out of the quota of money Ireland regularly furnished for the national treasury.

At the same time, the visit to Dublin she found memorable. She praised the Botanic Garden, one of the largest in Europe, and the Museum of Natural History, with its perfect skeleton of an 'Irish fossil Deer', and the models of buildings, monuments and bridges arranged for information and instruction. There were crowds there, from all walks of life. She noted an apprentice boy, a mechanic, mothers and children, and yet there was perfect silence.[2]

An anonymous journal preserved in the National Library of Ireland gives an account of Dublin about this period from the point of view of an educated Catholic,[3] a turner, who hoped eventually to make a career at the Bar, in the Kings Inns. 'F' – to whom he was secretly engaged – lived near the city centre, and used to spend the day walking in Leinster Lawn, in Merrion

---

1. Mrs T. Mitchell, *Gleanings from travels in England, Ireland and through Italy* [c. 1840], vol. 2, p. 7.
2. The 'Irish fossil Deer' is the Great Irish Elk.
3. *Journal of a Young Man with an account of Dublin social life, 1834-7.*

Square or in Stephen's Green, meeting friends, making acquaintances. On dull days, the large Georgian windows were a great aid to sociability – and to the sensitivities of a nervous courtship. Not only could the inmates look out, and engage friends in conversation, but the passerby on the street had a clear view of who was at home and decide whether this was a convenient time for calling. In the case of the lovely 'F', her courtier knew through her mimed messages when she was alone, without the embarrassing presence of Mamma or Papa.

The young diarist took an interest in some of the sensations of the day, such as the attempt on the life of Louis Philippe on January 1, 1837, and the execution of Patrick Martin and Maria Canning in 1834 for poisoning her husband, when, he wrote, the streets were 'a good deal crowded'. But otherwise his spare time was spent in going to lectures, plays or artisans' meetings or visiting the Dublin Society. He sometimes went steeplechasing, or attended races, but his tastes were mixed, enjoying the Practical Floral & Horticultural Show just as well as the Antiques at the Royal Hibernian Academy.

What he shared with Kate, whose Protestant background decreed a more restrained style of living, was an interest in theatre[4] and music, and in Loo, which was the popular card game in both their homes – and had been among the privileged classes for a century. Kate Cullen – in her quite separate Dublin – was taken to the pantomime by her brother Giles soon after her arrival in the capital, but, like her older woodturner contemporary, took more interest in the audience than in the performance. She remembered seeing Thomas Moore's sister – 'a little old lady, dressed in black velvet, with a red scarf about her, and her hair in short curls.' She saw Charles Keane and his wife, formerly Ellen Tree, acting at the Theatre Royal. But in her imagination she was with her sister Diana, who first saw the couple acting in *The Honeymoon* on their wedding night. The two actors had been married that morning, and all Dublin turned out in the evening to see the play. Kate also saw the famous Helen Faucit[5] as Rosalind in *As You Like It*.

The singers Kitzy remembered particularly were Mario and Grisi, who were husband and wife. Kate was to hear them in after years in London and the performances imprinted on her mind were those in *Norma* and *La*

---

4. He mentions in his journal the Mrs Waylett who was brought to Clare by the Stacpooles to entertain them at Stamer Park. One night at the theatre he was 'looking over box sheet, did not see anybody so took my seat at random. A very stupid night it would have been, but for Mrs Waylett, and she scarce redeemed it.' He visited the Kingscourt Private Theatre in 1834 and thought 'The little theatre is well got up. It requires only that the actors learn their parts better to render it very attractive.'

5. Portrayed as *Antigone* in watercolour, shortly afterwards, by the Clare artist, Frederick Burton. National Gallery of Ireland, cat. no. 2359.

Sonambula. 'It was said that when Jenny Lind afterward took the part of Norma, Grisi said 'There is but one Norma – that is Grisi'.'

> Another celebrity . . . was Robson, who used to sing 'Villikins and Dinah' in London. He began his career in Dublin. He was an ugly little red-haired man. The 'Olympic' used to be crowded night after night by people who went just to hear Robson sing this one song. He was dressed in a little green coat with a red handkerchief sticking out of his pocket.

The singing in St Patrick's earned the Cathedral the nickname 'Paddy's Opera'. The Robinson family were the principal performers, 'it was a real treat to hear them all in an anthem'. John was organist, William and Frank were tenors, and Joe sang bass.[6] Kate remembered Joe, William and Frank singing in the Antient Concert Rooms, as well as two other singers, father and son, named Smith.

The concerts given by the Philharmonic Society, she says, attracted younger audiences, because new songs were performed, and celebrities like Miss Dolby were invited over from London, while the older musiclovers preferred the concerts staged by the Anacreontic Society (named after the Greek poet Anacreon). Dublin at this time

> was a very pleasant place, and, during the season, many people came up from the country, amongst these were my sisters Mrs Faris (as she was then), who generally came up to hear the Italian Opera, and usually got some man like John Galway or William Kellett to accompany her and the sisters to the opera, or the concerts, and Bessie St Leger, who would often come to buy handsome dresses, furs and things of that kind unprocurable in the country.

Church provided another kind of entertainment, integral to Kate's life. John Gregg, who ran the Achill Mission, and afterwards was Bishop of Cork, was Rector of Trinity Church, Lower Gardiner Street, and considered to be the finest preacher in Dublin – 'certainly a wonderful preacher, very fascinating – very dull and lagging at first, he then warmed up as he went on. A favourite ending of his to a peroration was 'the blackness of darkness for ever'!' Kate heard him preach in Irish, and later, at meetings of the Irish Society, heard him give his addresses in the native tongue.

St Matthias's in Hatch Street was the Cullens' parish church, a handsome new building with Greek Corinthian portico, and a galleried interior

---

6.   According to W. H. Grindle, *Irish Cathedral Music, a history of music at the cathedrals of the Church of Ireland*, 1989, p. 71, William was a bass, John a tenor, and Joseph a baritone. John Robinson was organist at St Patrick's from 1829-43. The four brothers were noted for introducing German part-songs to Irish audiences.

St. Patrick's Cathedral, Dublin, from the Churchyard, 1793, by James Malton (c.1760–1803). (Photograph courtesy of the National Gallery of Ireland, no. 2620.)

St. Matthias's Church, Hatch Street, Dublin, c.1957. Built 1843 by Daniel Robertson.
(Photograph courtesy of the Representative Church Body Library, Dublin.)

with box pews, and Kate preferred its rector, Maurice Day – who also became a bishop – to the dramatic Gregg. At Sunday School, Kate was taught by a Miss Lefroy, whose footman used to carry a large box of books into the church every Sunday for children to borrow and take home with them. When she was older, she learned the Catechism – 'out of Archbishop Ussher's Catechism' – under the tutelage of John Gregg and she attended a Bible class, run by one of the curates of St Stephen's Church, the 'Pepper Pot', in Upper Mount Street.

For the Cullens, devotion rather than architectural uplift was the aim; and they tended to frequent the various chapels of ease about the city, where good sermons could be heard. Mr Krause at the Bethesda, in Dorset Street, was 'a first rate preacher, and a very good man', who had such a large following that it was almost impossible to get a seat in his church. 'Cultured' people favoured Dr Fleury of the Molyneux Church.[7] Mr Verschoyle of Baggot Street Church – which was regularly attended by members of the medical profession – was also famed for his piety. 'Called by his mother 'her sainted son', Kate agreed that 'indeed his face was very beautiful, and seemed to me always while in prayer to have a kind of halo over it.' Their cousin, Nellie Vandeleur, who was such a spiritual influence on Kate's mother, introduced Bidz to the saintly Mr Verschoyle, yet, Kate lamented, 'notwithstanding her acquaintance with dignitaries of the Church', Nellie 'gave up her allegiance to the Church afterwards, and threw in her lot with the Darbyites – dying in that faith'.

Some of the best preaching Kate heard was in Leeson Street, at the Magdalen Asylum. The unfortunates crowded into the gallery of the 18th century chapel to hear speakers such as Mr Lowe, Dr Singer and Mr Pollock – the names Kate remembered – as well as the celebrated Hugh MacNeill, who came over from England to preach at an institution.

> The sermon was very impressive, and, when it was over, a wail came from the Gallery where the inmates were, and one or two Gentlemen in the seat behind us whom we knew took out a handful of silver each, and put it into our hands to put on the plate; which we children were very proud to do.

> Hugh MacNeill was a magnificent-looking man – very tall – and, as he stood up in the pulpit in his black gown, his scarlet hood and his white hair, and pointed with his finger to emphasize what he was saying, the

---

7. In the case of William Le Fanu, on hearing the curate Reverend Henry Galbraith preaching at St Stephen's Church on 1 July, 1855 he 'resolved to change his way of life, to repent, and to turn to God', a conversion which lasted about a year to eighteen months. W. J. McCormack, *Sheridan Le Fanu and Victorian Ireland*, 1980, pp. 125-6.

words being, 'Only for you I wouldn't be here' – meaning the final
punishment of the poor victims – the effect was very great, and sent one
home very much impressed.

There was much religious discussion at home. Jemmy was always arguing
with Cousin Eliza Webb about who were the best preachers, or about Predestination and Election, and the opposing merits of Arminianism. Cousin Eliza,
widow of a clergyman, followed her husband in being a strong advocate of
Predestination but with this Jemmy could not agree.

Public speaking was as attractive an entertainment for the family as preaching and Kate and her mother used to go to O'Connell's meetings whenever
they could. What added to their interest was that O'Connell's great friend,
Tom Steele – who had sacrificed all his property to further the national cause
– came from an old Clare family. Often, while they lived in Percy Place, Kate
saw Tom Steele walking with the nationalist leader, or sometimes wandering
along by himself, stopping now and then to dip and wash his hands in the
canal.

Interior of St. Matthias's Chuch, Hatch Street, Dublin, 1843
(Photograph courtesy of the Representative Church Body Library, Dublin.)

Daniel O'Connell used to wear a blue Volunteer cloak when she saw him, and a cap with a gold band around it, and she remembered clearly the day he was liberated from prison, when he was paraded around Dublin in a triumphal car, attired in crimson velvet and gold, accompanied by his small grandson, and by an old Irish harper, who was playing Irish airs.

William Curran, brother of Robert Emmet's Sarah, was another character to be seen about Dublin, and she and her mother would meet him when out walking. He lived in Fitzwilliam Place.

> Mr Curran was a typical old gentleman of that period, wore a long light brown surtout, and a black tall hat, and a very high stock. On meeting my mother he would pull out his pocket book and say,

> "Glad to meet you, Mrs Cullen, as I can now find out what day I can have you to meet a few special friends. I shall send a note beforehand to remind."

> Invariably, the note came a day or two before, containing the invitation, and the words inscribed 'To remind'. The party was composed of savants and literary men of the day, all well known people.

There were no cabs at that period in Dublin, and the hack-cars, Kate recalled, were either covered cars, which were entered at the back, and were most uncomfortable, or outside cars

> like the present outside cars, but very uncouth. They were all very well for young men, but uncomfortable for ladies, and not considered quite the correct thing for them.

6

Dear Half-Remembered Ones

Donegal 1846-7

Kate was 13 years of age when her handsome vivacious brother, Paddy, became a cadet in the Indian army. During his tedious wait in the hope of some military appointment, he had approached an old friend of the family, Sir Robert Campbell, who had been under some obligation to Paddy's grandfather, the Reverend Carn Cross Cullen, and was now a Director of the East India Company. Bidz accompanied her son to London for an interview with the Board, and bought his outfit, and he sailed away from the London docks in an East Indiaman early in the spring of 1845.

Despite the initial anticipation and excitement, the voyage turned out to be monotonous. It was not a pleasant experience journeying around the Cape – a route which took three months. Paddy suffered from pernicious seasickness, and reached Calcutta on May 10 in a weak condition. Still his buoyant self, and elated at his arrival, he only longed for news of home. He wrote to Bidz the following day

> I have reported myself at the Fort, and am now under pay! I was greatly disappointed at not finding either a letter or newspaper from old Ireland, it would have been so easy to have directed it to Fort William. This certainly is a beautiful place, and justly called the 'City of Palaces'. We are all invited to the Governor's Ball, which is to be on the 24th. It will be rather hot work.

> We were very near, just at the end of our voyage, meeting with a sad accident. Our Pilot got drunk, and steered in such a manner as to very nearly knock the bottom out of the good ship, Tartar, as she struck the ground three times. 'Very pleasant' you will say.

He had not yet heard which regiment he would join, but thought he might apply for a regiment stationed at Cawnpore, so as to be near his 'dearly beloved Aunt' – Aunt Eliza Campbell. However, before he completed his letter, he learned that he had been ordered to join the 49th Bengal Native Infantry at Berhampore.

Paddy was ready to make the most of his new career. He could already speak Hindustani fluently; but 'it is really a great bore to wear uniform. . . .'

he grumbled. What was worse was the phenomenal cost of a garment for everyday wear, the short, tight-fitting shell-jacket. 'The fellow charges 16 rupees, 32 shillings. This is a most horribly expensive place, as old Gorman says, you must always have your hand on your penny.'

Paddy's letter, received in a flurry of pleasure at home, was copied out by Georgina in her best hand, and the copy sent to Janey in Sligo, to be pored over in the company of Bessie and her husband, Noblett.

It was probably the last letter the family had from him. Kate completes the tragic story in her memoir.

> He very soon was appointed to his Regt . . . and sailing up the Hoogly to join it took cholera and died in his Budgerow, before he could reach his destination, Berhampore. We never heard any particulars of his death at the time, and heard of it first from an Indian paper received by a Sligo lady. It was not till the year 1853 we heard any tidings of his last moments, and that from one of his brother officers who was with him when he died, a Mr Williams; he had sisters living in Dublin, who found out after a long time where we lived, through some cousins of ours whom they happened to come across. My mother had a nice letter from him sending her some of his hair, and a little seal and chain, and some letters, and a part of a Diary written on board ship.
>
> Poor fellow! he went off with every prospect of a brilliant career, in the highest spirits, and such was the termination of all. His death was a terrible blow to all of us, especially to my poor mother, who was so proud of him and expected such great things from him. I can well remember the sense of desolation and grief which as a child I felt the day the news of his death arrived, and wondering how the sun could shine so brightly when we were all so overwhelmed with sorrow.

Patrick Edmund was buried at Berhampore. Years later they heard, no doubt through the Glenade Cullens, that Aunt Eliza Campbell had been to see the grave.

About 1846, when she had finished at Miss Gregg's school, Kate Cullen spent a year with her sister Mary Labatt in Donegal. She had already visited Mount Charles, the parish of Kilcar, several times. She liked the people of Donegal, thought them good-looking and clever, and was appalled at the poverty they had to endure. '"Mess Ketsy", they called me', she writes.

> The people of Donegal were in those days altogether an Irish-speaking people (with very few exceptions). Some of them spoke nothing but Irish. When the car came near Killybegs, the children used to run out of the cottages calling out, 'Gim'me money, Gi'me money!'; and this was about all the English they knew. To this appeal we were supposed to respond as liberally a⌐ we felt disposed.

Page of manuscript memoir. Private collection, Dublin.

Mary Labatt used to dole out coloured petticoats and skirts to the people: she was greatly beloved by them.

Like other clergy families, the Labatts played a major part in alleviating the suffering during the Famine. Kate writes of Mary Labatt making soup in big boilers, and dealing it out to the poor, 'which kept the life in them in those dark days, when there was so little milk or any kind of food to be had.' Edward meanwhile raised contributions of meal from Lord Enniskillen, and the other country gentlemen he knew in Fermanagh and Donegal. He printed and distributed around Ireland, and across the water, circulars begging assistance, and raised large sums of money in this way. Writing at the end of the century, Kate still remembered the opening phrase of the circulars – 'Kilcar, a remote parish in the west of Donegal. . . .'

The country people earned a little money by knitting or working embroidered sprays in satin-stitch on muslin – 'this last being taught them at the time of the Famine by 'sprigging-masters' – as much for their own benefit as for that of the poor girls it was supposed to support,' was Kate's caustic comment.

> It, however, rescued many poor families from absolute want. My sister, Mary Labatt, took a prominent part in it. I have often seen her sitting up late at night drawing the patterns on muslin for the people, who would be all at the door waiting when we looked out in the morning. You would hardly believe that the hands you saw turn out this work could have produced it – the hands of those who had been at field-work all their lives.

> I have often watched them working at their hoops on the roadside. They certainly produced beautiful work, and my sister was an adept at it. The girls used to have a candle in turn, and, as many as could gather round it – we will say three or four – would 'sprig' by the light of it in one of the cottage rooms. Then, if one girl quarrelled with another, it was very usual to hear her say – 'You'll not sprig at my candle to-night!'

> While on this subject, I recall how, on one occasion, when out walking with some friends on the road where there was a sprigging party working, a young fellow who was with us made a rush at the girls, in a spirit of fun. The girls scattered as if in terror, and we passed on thinking that they understood it was a joke: but, on coming back that way, we were accosted by two men, one of whom kept saying – 'Yeh took the piece! Yeh took the piece.' While the other, I perceived, went up behind young Hume, and was just in the act of levelling a blow at him with a big heavy stick, when I rushed forward and seized it with both hands, before it descended with full force on his head. In all probability he would have been brained, but I was just in time.

Kate had obviously inherited the 'indomitable courage' of Great Grandmother Cullen.

> Next day the men came to the house to apologize, saying that one of the girls had lost her piece of work in the flight, and they had taken Mr

Hume for another young man, who was very unpopular: but they would not have done anything to injure 'the Widow Hume's Son', who was so good to the poor.

The Protestant clergy of the time have been criticised frequently for using the soup pots as a means for proselytising as much as for the relief of the starving, though it is also well known that many of the same clergy and landowners threw themselves selflessly into the fight to save the sick and the hungry, and a number of them lost their own lives to famine fever. Edward Labatt, while no doubt devoting himself with genuine altruism to caring for the less fortunate Catholics, took pride in a young convert, who stayed in his house, and who said that she had been won over to the Church of Ireland because of his preaching. Young Kate became cynical.

> There was a young lady staying at the Labatts, who pretended to turn Protestant, which game she carried on for a long time, both there, and after she went home. Her name was Maria Keane, and her twin sister, Ellie Keane, used to write heart-rending letters to her on the subject. Her mother also wrote her beautiful letters: and how she had the hardihood to persist in this game in the face of these letters I do not know. I too for a while believed in her, but I gave up the belief after some time: and I afterwards heard that she was attending Mass again, and finished her course by marrying a police officer, who was also a Roman Catholic. Labatt had made a great fuss about her having turned in his house, and by his preaching, and they kept her for some time in the house, and were very kind to her, but of course it all came to nothing.

Mr Lodge was Rector of a small church at Killybegs, on the hill above the busy fishing village. St Catherine's Rectory was some way beyond the town, a large plain Georgian house, reached by a drive under sparse trees, terminating in a magnificent view of the rocky promontory and the inlet of Killybegs.

Kate stayed here on occasions. Mrs Lodge she thought 'a nice old lady, but rather bitter.' The house was full of young 'well educated' boys, and four girls, among whom Letitia became her particular friend. Letitia accompanied her to England to stay with Georgina, after the latter married. To her sorrow, two of the younger boys died half-a-dozen years later, victims of one of the contemporary epidemics of typhoid or cholera. Alexander, the youngest, was 17, Richard was 23, and their plain headstones are to be seen forming a straight row with that of their parents in the little churchyard at Killybegs.

Fintra,[1] about a mile from Killybegs, was

---

1.   Fintra, or 'Fionn trá' is the Irish for 'fair' or 'white strand'.

the hospitable residence of Mrs Hamilton, her sons and daughters – a lovely spot, sheltering itself under the mountain – in front was a fine stretch of strand, on which the foamy waves came rolling in with a mighty roar. At the back a goodly belt of plantation added to the shelter. The common scarlet Fuchsia here nearly attained to timber, and had a fine effect.

The mountain, if I remember right, is called Largy: and from the road here was to be seen a view never to be forgotten – Donegal Bay with its vast expanse of water, the Sligo Mountains – Knocknarea and Benbulben – the Mayo mountains, etc. Labatt named this view the 'Amharc Mor' (the 'Grand View').[2]

She speaks also of the White House, residence of George Venables Wilson, agent to Mr Murray Stuart, one of the Donegal landowners. Mrs Wilson was a pleasant woman, and her husband 'famous for telling wonderful stories about quantities of fish he had caught and game he had bagged.' She remembered a week there when there were several parties, with the Lodges and Edward Labatt in attendance at most of them.

Famine times had a happy consequence for Kate's fourth sister, Georgina Frances, who was staying in Sligo while Kate was in Kilcar. John Elliott, a Lieutenant in the Royal Marines, sailed in to Donegal in a frigate laden with meal for the starving population. He went across to Sligo to a ball, where he saw Georgina, fell in love with her, and proposed for her the next day. They were married on April 1, 1847, and lived a long, eventful life together, until she died in 1907, and he some years later, at Plymouth.

Jack and Georgina remained Kate's close friends throughout their days. Her brother-in-law, Edward, on the other hand, despite the fun she had with him as a youngster, she disapproved of as soon as she was old enough to make a judgement. She blamed him for Mary's early death.

Poor thing! she died[3] . . . of influenza, and I fear he took no trouble to keep her alive. Withheld all nourishment, which is so necesssary in that disease. Staying in the house he had a Miss Whitelaw, whom he afterwards married, and who kept him in fine order and submission till he died after a good many years a very decrepit old man.

Perhaps it was the remaining members of the Cullen family who placed the handsome marble memorial on the wall of Manorhamilton Church –

---

2. Kate, who knew Irish, wrote the word in Irish characters in her manuscript. 'Amharc' is the Donegal word for 'scene' or 'sight'.
3. Kate writes 'in the year 1872'; but the date on the memorial in Manorhamilton Church is 1864.

To Mary Jane
beloved & devoted wife of Rev Edward Labatt
Rector of Kilcar Co. Donegal
& private chaplain to Earl of Enniskillen
eldest daughter of Lt Col. Cullen.
died Easter morning 1864, aged 50 Years.

Always ready to administer to the wants of the poor.

7

Darkening to the Sun

Leitrim and Maryborough 1848

The Famine was the inadvertent cause of notions of marriage entering Kate's head. Her mother had at last been persuaded to move to Maryborough (now Port Laoise), to keep house for Giles, Kate and Jemmy moving with her. But Kate went first for a prolonged visit to Carrick-on-Shannon, to stay with Diana at Shannon Lodge.

Diana Faris naturally drew young men to her. She was beautiful, warm, charming. There were many strangers in Carrick in 1848, brought there by the Board of Works in connection with various famine relief schemes in the Shannon area, which included the building of three new bridges, at Carrick, Shannonbridge and Athlone. Three engineers employed on the Carrick job, Gisborne, Ford and Ottley, were frequent visitors at the Lodge, and became intimate friends of the Farises: and in their company came two paymasters from the Army Commissariat attached to the relief works, James Long and John Ramsay McCulloch.

James Long and his friend felt welcome within the walls of Shannon Lodge, a home from home. Soon James was courting Kate's bosom friend Anna Kirkwood. Kate herself fell in love with the tall, handsome Scotsman, McCulloch, in his blue uniform with the black rebut facings. Their courtship was rapid, not altogether approved by her family, because he was only a Deputy Assistant Commissary General (DACG), one rung above a mere clerk. He had been in the army about four years, received his promotion while in Canada, and like James Long hoped for another promotion in two years, though James waited patiently for it before proposing to Anna.

John McCulloch was likeable, kindly, and indolent, sometimes even dis-solute; content to drift along, managing the regiment provisions, paying and negotiating transport, doling out wages, acting as general dog's body. One note to Kate, in the initial stages of their courtship, apologises that it will be eight o'clock in the evening before he has finished paying, and he asks to be excused from some arrangement. Another explains his reluctance to spend a day with Diana's friend, Bennett Little – 'To tell the truth I hate going to a strange House, therefore do not ask me.' His duties took him to Ballinamore on the far side of Leitrim, among other places, so that their meetings had to be sporadic. Yet he was deeply attached to the small red-headed 17-year-old,

Shannon Lodge, Carrick-on-Shannon. (Photograph courtesy of Shane Flynn.)

not so beautiful as her sister, but possessing her own dynamism. He liked the easy manners of the Irish, and decided to grow his hair long.

They enjoyed the occasional 'pic-nic' together, and dancing – which Kate loved – and her beau was attentive with gifts and affectionate verses. In the summer of 1849, before his departure to London and his posting to the West Indies, he proposed marriage.

Jack, as she now called him, on his return to London, found himself sole occupant of the family home – 'a big house turned upside down at my disposal' – while his people were away in the country. He had seen one sister off to Argyleshire and Edinburgh, and she, in looking for some way in which to have certain letters redirected discreetly to her, had had to confide in him. 'This great secret was *Love*', and he, who had not yet divulged the matter of his engagement to anyone, confided in her. 'Such a pair of fools is beyond my description – as we made of ourselves.'

'The Governor' was a formidable figure. Author of a well known contemporary work on political economy, as well as of a geographical dictionary,[1] he was impatient with his unambitious son. They had met twice since Jack's return. He has been 'in great glee at my coming home & I am in great glee at seeing him in such good spirits', so obviously Jack did not wish to upset such good humour straightaway.

A week later – just a few days before he was due to set sail for the West Indies – he broke the news of his engagement to his parents, and they were very pleased, feeling that Jack now had a stimulus to save, and 'become a respectable member of society'. 'The Governor has put a very severe test on me. He says I must pay all my debts just to show him that I really am determined to alter my course, by turning over a new leaf', and he asked Kate to pass the message of his good intentions on to her mother. His own mother regretted Kate wasn't older, because she thought Jack would never be able to look after himself, and could Kate be trusted? 'You have no idea Kate how they laughed at me when I got home: called me an Irishman & a barbarian. All my whiskers have [been] cut & the pert little come toos have very nearly disappeared. Poor me! I am obliged to be on my P's and Q's.'

While the family organised themselves to send Kate 'an invite', cholera had driven many people out of London (it was in Sligo too though it hadn't yet reached Carrick). 'It is most frightful', Jack wrote from Barnes, where he and the family were staying;

---

1. John Ramsay McCulloch (1789-1864) was the first Professor of Political Economy at London University; and from 1838 until his death was Controller of the Stationery Office. He published obsessively, essays and books about statistics and commerce and other practical subjects, the most important being *A Dictionary, Practical, Theoretical and Historical, of Commerce and Commercial Navigation*, 1832, and a geographical, statistical and historical dictionary in two volumes, in 1841.

upwards of 10,000 have died from it alone in London & vicinity – it was on the increase last week, but fortunately has decreased a little this week, altho' the deaths this last week were 273 cholera & 46 diarrhoea, that was up to the 7th Sept. Every person who can leave town has left. I never saw such a deserted place as London is at present. You do not see one carriage for every hundred.

As soon as he returned to London, Jack had two copies of his likeness taken at the Polytechnic, and Christina McCulloch forwarded the better one to Kate, with a polite note telling her that all the family agreed that it was a 'very true likeness'. He himself wrote from Southampton, where he was now with his brother Henry and a friend, in good spirits. He had a good berth on the 'Avon', and thought the coming voyage would last about 17 days – six or seven to Madeira, and the remainder to Barbados.

The 'Avon' had reached Madeira by September 24, here it deposited passengers and mail and Jack wrote from a rolling ship, briefly sick in a blowing gale. The soldiers were not allowed to go on shore because they had come from a cholera–stricken country. Madeira was a beautiful island, very romantic – 'Just the place to pass a 'honeymoon' if the passage was not so long.' He could see some of the passengers purchasing hats and canary birds from the little boats nearby, and the air was filled with the regular boom of cannons, as they fired guns every five minutes from the citadel and fort, commemorating the anniversary of Don Pedro's death.

The voyage continued smoothly, and on October 10 the ship came upon what Naipaul has described as 'the bright, shocking, beautiful picture' of Barbados.[2] The island was small and flat, 21 miles long, and surrounded by coral reefs: the next island, St Vincent, about 100 miles to the east. The view Jack had was of beaches and plains rising in a series of terraces to a low mountain, Hillaby. Ruins of old burnt out estate houses were scattered through the pale sugar cane groves; and the mahogany, palm and bread fruit trees were full of monkeys, chirping sparrows and tree frogs, which piped and whistled all night long.

This was to be Jack's centre for the next 18 months. 'At this time of the year it looks very pretty indeed', he said, 'everything is so fresh & green, and if the roads had any other appearance but white the place would appear more cool & comfortable than it is.'

But he found Trafalgar Square 'miserable in the extreme' – not even as large as the modest sized square in front of the St George's house, – the big house in the small town of Carrick-on-Shannon where Jack and Kate had met and courted.

---

2.   *The Enigma of Arrival*, 1986, p. 136.

Also the inhabitants of Bridgetown, 'all manners of colours' as he put it, were hard to take. He told Kate, 'I could not describe the dress of these people to you at all at all [he fell easily into the Irish expression when addressing her]. It is generally all white, white head dress, & black face & feet. You can imagine how absurd it looks'. Later when he was ill, he became convinced that this country was no place for the 'white man'. 'Niggers', he said bitterly, ' – they are nothing more than a species of monkey, without tails, something like the Isle of Man cats – they have no tails.'

This deep-rooted racial prejudice, stemming no doubt from his upbringing, seemed to flare up in an unhappy situation. In Ireland he had been happy to enjoy a greater social freedom and to wear 'long hair' in the company of the Cullens, but he quickly conformed to the habits of his social strata when he returned home to England, and it is interesting to ponder at this point on whether he could have settled with Kate who had played with beggars, and still cared for the more intriguing characters.

It is true that Kate herself had strong prejudices, but these were mainly in the areas of manners and morals. We have no evidence of any marked racial or social prejudice. Reared in West of Ireland society, which still manifested vestiges of the Gaelic clan system, class and cultural differences were not nearly so divisive, but tended to be respected.

Kate, as he wrote to her, was having an entertaining time, dancing with Cousin Andy Stacpoole at the Royal Irish Yacht Club in Kingstown, and visiting her other Clare relatives at their home soon afterwards. His letter of November 28, 1849, which did not reach her till January 1, 1850, had more alarming news to report. His chief officer, Mr Price, who had gone on the tour of inspection, died of yellow fever after about six hours of illness; and he had been buried at Dominica the same evening. His son had set out to meet him on his return.

> I was sitting on the verandah waiting to see them pass & welcome the old fellow back again, when to my horror & amazement Mrs Price came rushing up to me crying. . . . I was never so shocked in all my life. . . . The Old Man was such a kind & efficient officer. . . . I was young Price's best man in Montreal. Yellow fever is raging in Antigua & 27 men 1 woman & an officer died the other day. All the other islands are healthy.

Jack's letters constantly lamented the dullness and monotony of West Indian life, and complained about the sloth of the postal service in delivering Kate's letters from Ireland. One would suspect that Kate's affections were cooling, such was the distance between them, were it not that she numbered his letters meticulously as they arrived, and she read all eagerly.

Her fiancé filled the time off duty playing cricket or reading the latest novels by Dickens; and he had a delightful trip to St Thomas and Martinique.

But the climate of Barbados certainly did not suit him. Nor did that of Berbice, his next appointment. He had to smoke to keep the mosquitoes off – 'one mass of bites, can only scratch & bear it.' In August 1850 he was moved from the Fort Camp of Berbice to Demarara, where he was a victim to fever, followed by a relapse with ague in addition to fever.

> Have you ever had ague? It is certainly the most horrid thing imaginable. Fancy in a country like this for heat being in one's bed covered with Blankets, shivering & shaking & one's teeth knocking against one another [as] if you had just come out of iced water & then followed by such a burning fever! . . . I can imagine very well now a Lady fainting. I know that if anything particular happened to me, since I have had these attacks, that my nerves fail me altogether & I am all flutter & shakes.

This is the last letter to Kate that survives, a distressful morbid communication. Kate had told him that she was about to move back to Dublin, leaving Maryborough because Giles was getting married; and Jack couldn't understand why she wasn't thrilled. He was slightly sarcastic.

> In Dublin you have twice the chances of going to Carrick – & then when there to see Victor [Mr St George's agent, who flirted with Kate's sister Diana] in the latest costume! Only imagine! We must put Shannon Lodge & its inmates in the background altogether when Victor is there – Mr Every Lady.

The acid humour, the feverish tones, reflect his understandable frustration and depression, the experience of so many Europeans forced to follow their professions into unhealthy climes during the last century. Jack's health had deteriorated badly, his morale was very low. It was about this time that Kate, now nearly 20, was persuaded to break off their engagement.

We have no record of how he bore the blow but a year or so afterwards he resigned his commission, never having gained the promotion he was due.

Kate, looking back in her *Memoir* from the distance of 50 years, wrote about him in a dispassionate way.

> He was a very nice fellow, but on going abroad afterwards became, I am sorry to say, rather dissipated, and I was advised to break off the engagement: which I did. I never saw him again. He died while still a young man – I think abroad. Had he married me instead of waiting for promotion, he might have had a better fate and been saved from the bad influences under which he fell.

But she kept his letters for the rest of her life, the blue envelopes tied in a bundle with a strip of sprigged muslin.

8

The Playing Fields of Earth

Maryborough, Dublin, Sligo 1848-60

Kate told Jack McCulloch something about the sociable life she had been leading since he went away. She met his brother David, touring in Donegal, and he had spent a day in Maryborough with her mother and Giles, who 'pronounced him a very nice fellow'. She thought he looked very like Jack.

But she may not have told Jack everything. It was while living in Maryborough that Kate's affections strayed – was this the real reason for breaking off her engagement? – and she formed another attachment.

She and Dr Burton met while playing cards. The Resident Magistrate in Maryborough was a Mr Cannon, who lived at Portrane, with his wife and children, and his wife's mother, who was a daughter-in-law of the renowned United Irishman, Napper Tandy. Kate had mixed feelings about the company. Mrs Tandy was the one Kate remembered with approval among the clan – 'a nice old lady'.

> Every evening of our lives, the car was brought out and we were driven up to Portrane to spend the evening playing cards. The game was 'Loo', which I shirked playing on many occasions, never being an enthusiast at cards or attaining any proficiency thereat. The Governor of the Asylum at Maryborough was a Dr Thomas Burton, who was one of the Clare Burtons, and a Cousin of Sir Frederick Burton, the painter of the 'Blind Girl at the Well'.[1] Dr Burton was a very cultured man, and a very good doctor. He was often at the Cannons, and often at our house, and I became engaged to him; but the engagement after some time was broken off. He was much older than I was.

The attachment may have been engineered by Bidz, who had been treated successfully by Dr Burton for asthma. Kate was no doubt attracted to the urbane man – the glamour of his cousin the famous painter certainly appealed

---

1. 'The Blind Girl at the Holy Well: a scene in the West of Ireland' – shown by Burton at the Royal Hibernian Academy in 1840 – was engraved for circulation almost immediately and became very popular. It seems to have caught Kate Cullen's imagination, and it is likely that the Cullens, or Dr Thomas Burton, had a copy of the print.

the Rector - a very old man). The Cannons lived at a place called
"Portrane". Mrs. Cannon was a daughter of Mrs. Tandy whose
husband, Major Tandy, was a son of the famous Napper Tandy. Mrs
Tandy lived with her daughter, Mrs. Cannon. She was a nice old
lady but I do not think her grandchildren were nice to her. My
mother was always very attentive to her from an innate sense of
politeness which virtue I may remark was not of much account in
the Cannon family. The old lady was very fond of a game of cards.
I had no particular liking for any of the Cannons. They were all
married at this time except Henrietta and her brothers Harry and
Eddy. I liked Harry, I should say, and poor Eddy, who was a
great sufferer from asthma. Every evening of our lives the car
was brought out and we were driven up to Port-Naul to spend the
evening playing cards. The game was "Loo", which I shirked playing
on many occasions, never being an enthusiast at cards or attaining
any proficiency thereat. The Governor of the Asylum at Maryborough
was a Dr. Thomas Burton, who was one of the Clare Burtons, and a
Cousin of Sir Frederick Burton, the painter of the "Blind Girl at
the Well". Dr. Burton was a very cultured man, and a very good
doctor. He was often at the Cannons and often at our house and I
became engaged to him, but the engagement after some time was broken
off. He was much older than I was. He was a nephew by marriage
of the late Sir Henry Marsh and helped him a good deal in his

                                                          profession

Typed page of memoir. Private collection, Dublin.

to her – and the doctor would have been taken by her youth and vivacious
spirit. But it was clearly not a love match, as it had been in the case of poor
aimless Jack; and 'it must be confessed he did not quite come up to the high
estimate I had formed of his character.'

Kate describes her suitor as a travelled man, brought up in France where
he became a fluent speaker of French and other languages. He was appointed
Physician-in-Ordinary to Prince Woronzov, and Secretary of Legation to the
Russian Embassy at the Persian Court. His job in Persia had been to act as

interpreter at banquets and entertainments. He was conscious of the drabness of his formal English dress 'beside the gorgeous uniforms of Russia, blazing with jewels and gold lace, or the artistic dress of the East, the embroidered coat and crimson fez. His dress clothes, in addition to their ugliness, had become too tight for him. . . .'

Thomas Burton had spent many years at Dr Stevens Hospital in Dublin, as resident physician, and acted as assistant to Sir Henry Marsh, who was his uncle by marriage. Kate learned some gossip about the notorious Sir Henry.

> Sir Henry used to go flaunting about Dublin in his light carriage, driven by Peter Noone, his coachman, who occupied a high box seat, and was the terror of Dublin with his furious driving. Sir Henry was a little, light man. He was marrried to Mrs Arthur of Ennis, a widow, to whose sons he had been tutor. She was Dr Burton's aunt.

> The story is told that he admired her daughter, and asked for her in marriage. Mrs Arthur asked him in return, placing two decanters before him, one full and the other empty, 'Which will you have?' He replied, 'The full one'. This meant herself with her possessions; and Marsh gave up the daughter, and married the mother. She was much older than he was, and became stout and unwieldy, and more or less of an invalid, and spent most of her time in bed.

> After her death he married another widow, Mrs Kemiss of Shane Castle, Queen's Co. (She had been a Miss Jelly.) A station was built on the S & W Line near Shane Castle for the convenience of Sir Henry, who came down from Dublin every Saturday, to spend Sunday at Shane, the marriage being kept secret for years on account of the old gentleman's (Mr Kemiss) Will, by which his widow was forbidden to marry till her son was of age.

Kate felt that the Cannon family paid the Cullens great attention 'not I think on acount of our own attractions, but to make up their card party every night, and to secure the company of my brother Giles.' They were successful on both scores. The table was full for their card games, and Giles married the infatuated daughter in 1851.

Kate and her mother returned to Dublin. 'We took up our carriages,' she says, 'sorry to leave Maryborough for various reasons. It was a cheap place to live in and suited us very well on that account. Chickens, eggs, butter and things of that kind were cheaper than in any place I ever knew, and the house we had was also cheap. It was a very nice house, not very large, but big enough for us.'

However they had accepted that, when Giles married, they were to leave. They found lodgings in Dublin with an Englishwoman, in Upper Leeson Street. One of the sons of the Rector of Carrick, Robert Percy, lodged in the same house, and let Kate practice on his piano: and so the winter of 1851-2 passed by.

Mrs Arthur turned out to be rather disagreeable, and they next moved two doors down to the corner house next to the canal, which belonged to a Dr Dwyer. The house was healthy and airy, and their rooms had a fine view down the canal, and they stayed here for six or seven months until they heard that the Elliotts were coming home. Then they all shared a large house in the fashionable area, in Waterloo Road, and were there for the Great Exhibition in 1853. Queen Victoria opened it:

> Everyone wore white. The Queen wore a white worked muslin dress, and a white silk mantilla trimmed with fringe, made more as a scarf, and dropping back from the shoulders. They were greatly worn. The Queen [also] wore a pink bonnet which played the deuce with her complexion, as she had a very high colour.

> There was a déjeuner at the Yacht club, followed by a dance. The Queen came in her Yacht to Kingstown, and Lord St Germains, who was Lord Lieutenant, kept her waiting, for which crime she was plainly seen to give him a fine dressing. This I greatly resented, as he was a splendid looking man, very like my Father, the same features. The Queen declared the exhibition open, and for that whole year everyone went there nearly every day.

> There was a fine collection of pictures borrowed from all the old family places in Ireland. The original of Sir Frederick Burton's 'Blind Girl' was exhibited there.[2] The Exhibition building was in the Leinster Lawn, a wooden building covered with calico. There was a beautiful hall in the centre, where the beauty and fashion of Dublin used to pace up and down up to 4 and 5 o'c in the evening.

Kate, as usual, was watching the people, and enjoying the flirtations that took place in the roof galleries, where the promenading also went on. Everyone was dressed in the height of elegance. She herself wore a light striped silk dress, and with it a violet coloured silk cape, trimmed with rows of black lace, and with deep flounces of lace all around. Or she would wear one of her prettiest muslin dresses.

One of the highlights of the season was the Royal Marine Soirée, on December 2, 1853. Kate's little blue and gold programme prints the titles of 22 dances in all, among them the waltz from Faust, the Hibernian Quadrille and the Prince of Wales Galop. She was much in demand, taking the floor

---

2. The watercolour original was lent to the Dublin International Exhibition by Lt-General Sir George D'Aguilar (see W. G. Strickland, *A dictionary of Irish artists*, 1913, repr. 1969, vol. 1, pp. 131, 136.)

Queen Victoria and Prince Albert in the Paintings and Sculpture Hall of the Great Exhibition in Dublin, 1853, by James Mahony (1810–1879). (Photograph courtesy of the National Gallery of Ireland, no. 7009.)

both with men in uniform and with their civilian friends. She danced the first polka with her brother-in-law, Captain Jack Elliott, and after that had her choice of himself, Harry Lane or Jack Kaffir as partner. Just short of 21, radiant and petite, with the Cullen auburn hair, she was footsore and happy.

About this time, her brother Johnny Marcus emigrated to America, with no immediate object in mind. Walking down a street in Newark, New Jersey, he saw the name 'Toler' over the shop door of an iron foundry. Like so many Irishmen before and since, he took a chance on the familiar name – that of the Cullen's nurse in Skreeney, and straightaway found himself with a job as bookkeeper to his old nurse's son. Anne Toler was delighted to see one of the family, to sift over old times and to exchange the latest news, and she died three weeks later.

The Exhibition over, Kate went to England for about two years with her sister Georgina, and Jack Elliott. Captain Elliott was stationed at Woolwich, and lived in the Marine Barracks. Kate, as always, enjoyed herself to the full:

> I fell into a vortex of balls and parties. There was a lovely Ball at Chatham, lots of dancing. There were very ugly girls in Chatham. There were nice soirées given at the Royal Hospital, Greenwich: no style, but lots of dancing and a splendid band. There were Artillery Balls at Woolwich, also Artillery Soirées, which were extremely pleasant, music and all very good.

The Elliotts next went recruiting in the midlands, and Kate stayed on at Woolwich with a Colonel and Mrs Payne. Colonel Payne's grandfather was one of a band of young Irishmen who had bound themselves by an oath to protect Marie Antoinette during the French Revolution. Marie Antoinette had given him a ring, greatly treasured by the family: but, to their consternation, his mother, in a fit of frenzy, had thrown the heirloom into the sea. Kate became very fond of the Paynes, and particularly of Mrs Payne, one of an old Irish family, the Trants, who had settled in France; and later Mrs Payne became godmother to Kate's daughter.

Her next move was to Burton-on-Trent, where she rejoined the Elliotts, lodging in a hotel. Some members of the Bass and Allsop families – the brewers – made them welcome while they stayed there, and introduced them to the surrounding countryside, and they spent several evenings at a beautiful house near Burton, owned by cousins of Sir Robert Peel.

The Peels, Kate found, were snobs, and looked down on the beer families. Kate didn't approve of such superiority at all! She enjoyed the Allsops. Mrs Allsop was Irish – a Miss Towell from Limerick – and a character. At one déjeuner at her own house, she appeared in a sixpenny muslin and drank Guinness's stout – to Kate's delight: but she was equally capable of staging a grand dinner party.

More serious matters elbowed rudely into the frivolous pattern of life.

Without a moment's notice, Jack Elliott found himself called suddenly to the Crimea. Georgina – a grass widow for the time being – returned to Dublin with Kate, and shortly afterwards set off to visit the Labatts and the Lodges in Donegal, and her Sligo sister, Bessy St Leger. Kate's own life revolved as before between the parties of Dublin and the quieter sociability of Sligo until, in the late 50s, her mother Bidz said farewell to Dublin, and took a house on Sligo's Mall, near Bessy. It was a move that suited Jemmy, still a bachelor, with a strong bent for horticulture. He had a large strip of land in the Cullen's new domain, and charge of the St Leger's garden, which produced the most magnificent strawberries.

'I do not say these latter influenced his choice of residence', Kate relates with a twist of humour,

> but he was a good gardener, a taste he inherited from my father, who understood the culture of all those old-fashioned plants, such as pinks, crocuses, hyacinths, etc., which I am glad to say are still showing to the front as favourites. Jemmy was very useful as an adviser to Bessie and gave her a great deal of his time, which was a pleasure to him, as gardening was his greatest amusement.

Sligo was a thriving sea-port at this period, preserving reminders of its medieval prosperity in the street names it still boasts – such as Wine Street and Ship Street. Bessie's husband, Noblett St Leger, as town engineer was responsible for much of the most recent building.[3] Their house was a centre of sociability. The young Johnstons were visitors at the Mall nearly every day, and cards were still the favourite entertainment. The table was brought out every evening.

> I remember a game they played called 'Pope Joan', which I thought great fun. Doctor Little and some of the others were great whist players, and this ended by taking the lead of all the games and wiping out my favourite and that of many of the young people, 'Pope Joan'. Whist again gave way to chess, and I think this had the longest run.

Kate found Dr Little delightful. He was very musical, and, when cards palled and the piano lid was laid open for the entertainment of the company, he would sing a charming counter tenor to her alto in popular duets – 'I saw

---

3   St Leger fell out with the town architect, Benson, who shortly afterwards departed for Cork, so that only St Leger's name appears on the bridge they designed together (Victoria, now Hyde, Bridge). Even before that, the town had had aspirations to style, when the German architect, Cassels, had arrived to build the austere Hazelwood House for Colonel Wynne, and to design St John's Church on the lines of an early Roman basilica. Some of the windows of the church had been altered before Kate's time, and she lived to see further alterations of Cassel's building in 1883, when a chancel replaced the original apse.

from the beach', 'Dost thou remember', 'I know a bank'. She records an amusing family who used to come to Bessie's evenings, the Browns. Tom Brown was Clerk of the Peace and his daughter, Sara, was known as 'Tiddy-Oddy'.

> Tom Brown was a little man, and was rendered nearly invisible as he entered the room at a party by the wide crinolines of his wife and daughter on each side of him. Sara wore the crinoline long after it had disappeared off the legs of society (greatly to the relief of many). She was, I think, the last person to wear it in Sligo.

Another local character she remembered at the St Leger parties was the brother of the late patriot, Thomas Davis. An elderly man, Mr Davis had been a surgeon in the artillery and

> used to dance in the fashionable style of the day to such a pitch that we used to say his breath was so exhausted from his exertions that his life was hanging on a thread. From this he was called by the flippant Cullens, 'Hanging-on-a-thread', and went by that name in our family.

Soon after Kate's move to Sligo, Diana's rejected admirer, the eccentric Bennet Little, took it into his head to marry Sarah Percy, one of the daughters of the eccentric Rector of Carrick. Then Kate's friend, Tom Johnston, left Sligo. He had joined the army and they met in Waterloo Road – shortly before he sailed – as he was passing through Dublin to join his regiment. In old age she wrote of him, with regret. He was a handsome, clever young man. 'Poor fellow', she lamented, 'he did not live long after he went to India'.

Georgina's world was totally upturned. Her dearly loved Jack had been left for dead after the Battle of Malakoff. His servant, Pierce, mercifully found him and the story went round the family that half of Jack's sword was found on the field of battle, 'stuck in a fellow. He himself had the handle. He pulled out the other half, and had the two joined together again into one, and killed many a fellow with it, for years after.'

Jack and Georgina, to every one's joy, were happily reunited and Jack's new posting was to Ascension, where they were very anxious that Kate, now nearly 28, should join them, for a prolonged visit. It was a lonely place, and they urged her to come and entertain them, sending money for her outfit. She shopped in Dublin and Sligo for the lightest clothing she could find, under-clothing and dresses of cool materials; and very thin stockings without heels, which she bought in dozens, to use both on the voyage and on the Island. She had been warned that the heat would be excessive.

> It was all arranged that I should go in a sailing vessel which would touch at Ascension; but when all was ready I discovered that the 'Industry' was not going by Ascension after all, but I would have at first to take a

long trip by sea and only reach Ascension on the vessel's return voyage. I considered the journey too long, and decided to wait till the next voyage. But in the meantime I became engaged to Michael Mitchell, Manager of the Bank in Carrick-on-Shannon, and was married on the 26th April, 1860.

When the boat arrived in Ascension, I was not, of course, on board, and my sister Georgina said the disappointment of finding I had not come after all was the greatest she ever had. The Chaplain at A., who had seen my photograph, used to enquire at every boat if Mrs Elliott's sister was on board, and I suppose that his disappointment was almost equal to Georgina's.

The next letter brought the news of my marriage.

9

Only in Clay the Root of Love

Sligo and Carrick-on-Shannon before 1860

Kate's ultimate choice of a matrimonial partner was a logical one for an Irish girl of her time. Michael Mitchell's family, like Kate's, had been in Ireland since the 17th century. He came of legal stock, settled in Parsonstown, as it was fashionable to call Birr at the time, in King's County (Offaly). His father, George Mitchell, who had made an advantageous marriage with Susan Langstaff of Longfield, Co Meath, was Secretary to the County Grand Jury, and bequeathed this position to his eldest son, Thomas, who, in turn, held it until his death. The second son, Adam, was the remarkable member of the family, eight years older than Michael, and patriarchal in disposition. It was he who inherited the family home, Walcot, in Parsonstown. Solicitor to the Grand Jury, and later Crown Solicitor in King's County, he resigned these positions to his own son Thomas shortly before he died.

Michael was the tenth of 11 children. Two sisters died as infants, and of the other four, only Susan married, when in her early 30s. One brother emigrated to Australia. James and Michael went into the Bank, while Thomas and Adam remained in Parsonstown – a solicitor, and a doctor. They were a close-knit family, and Walcot Lodge, a charming old-world house close to the entrance gate of Birr Castle, at the end of the tree-lined Mall, was the Mitchell gathering-place.

Michael was 36 when he first courted Kate, and extremely eligible. He admitted to having already had several affairs. Kate mentions in her *Memoir* that he had been engaged twice before he paid his attentions to her. He was well-built, good-looking, had brown eyes, auburn hair and whiskers, and a winning personality. His ready sense of humour appealed to Kate and, as far as her family were concerned, his secure position in the Provincial Bank of Ireland in Carrick-on-Shannon meant there could be no opposition.

He was naturally religious, at 15 reading the Old Testament lesson in Birr Church at Matins on Sunday. He enjoyed poetry and popular ballads. As a young man he copied out some verses in praise of an uncle who had died young, written by a local balladeer named Larry Tristram about 1792. Rather stumbling doggerel, the acrostic form featured the letters making up Thomas Mitchell's name at the beginning of each line, so that his name could be read vertically: and this Mitchell love of ballad wit perpetuated itself in Michael's daughter Susan, writing her political satire 60 years later.

As well as verbal agility, Michael enjoyed a good life, in younger days being celebrated as the life and soul of balls and parties, and an agreeable flirt. He was reprimanded good-humouredly by his spinster sisters, who eagerly demanded full accounts of his dancing exploits. Sarah was understanding and tolerant. She wrote to him from Oxmantown Place in Parsonstown when he was in the bank in Sligo[1] –

> I am quite pleased that you tell me of all your amusements. I believe we are intended for sociability & I am glad that you always appear to relish the company of ladies. Indeed it made us all laugh to think they have so often made you a 'Victim' but I think it highly possible that their cruelty was merely the effect of your own 'heartless flirtations'.

Gentle Sarah – who merely hoped that he would 'never trifle with the affections of women', and who died unmarried aged 35 the following year – found her pleasures in lively nephews, and in writing devotional verses. Her life centred round the local church. 'Reading for my Sunday School classes & amusing myself with all the children of my acquaintance forms the happy business of my life', she told Michael.

> This town has just got rid of a set of missionary Priests who did nothing for the last month but confess & absolve the whole surrounding neighbourhood of Papists. I hear that this indulgence will extend for a period of seven years – May God deliver our county from all false doctrine & make us all Protestants & Catholics to know that if any Man has not the Spirit of Christ that he is none of his & that if he ask the Holy Spirit He will be given to us.

Thomas, Michael's eldest brother, who never married either, was a different kettle of fish. A typical Protestant and Unionist of his time, dour, exact-minded, he was like the rather leaden cousins to whom his poet niece Susan would take exception when she was living in Parsonstown years later. Writing to Michael at the Bank in Dungannon, on December 22, 1845, in neat solicitor's script, Thomas's news of Parsonstown was tinged with cynicism. Fresh from a pleasant trip to England, he had little sympathy towards the people of his own country, whom he described as 'dirty (filthy I must say)'. He spoke of a local clerk who had such self assurance he could push himself anywhere; of how the local Grandees had called upon the new accountant in spite of the fact that his wife was a Roman Catholic. The letter is bitter and crabbed. Thomas, no doubt, was frustrated by the limitations of the small town of Parsonstown and lonely, since there was no one in the old

---

1. Sarah Mitchell to Michael Thomas Mitchell, September 1852.

house but his mother, his sisters Jane, Margaret and Sarah, and himself. He ended his Christmas letter with news of local land disturbances. Lord Rosse was withstanding the rent protest staged by his tenants.

> There was a great sensation produced here today by the driving and Sale for Rent of a large quantity of Stock belonging to Lord Ross's tenants in Egish. I understand, but cannot state it as a fact, that he dismissed all the people who are in the habit of working at the Castle, on Saturday last, with the Exception of Gibbons – it is said to be his Lordship's intention to go live in Yorkshire, he had been so disgusted with the conduct of his tenantry, who have refused to pay any Rent, tho' having ample means – the Stock were all sold, but bought by the owners. I should not be surprised if some of the Tipperary Boys, would take vengeance on his Lordship or Geo Heman but trust nothing of the kind shall happen to either – if they happened to be in Tipperary, there can be little doubt of the result.

Michael like his brother witnessed the threat of violence close at hand. Among his papers he preserved two missives, addressed from the Molly Maguires – the flying column acting on behalf of the poorer, and defenceless tenantry – to two land agents, friends of his in Carrick-on-Shannon. Both letters make reference to the Frenchman who had inviegled himself into the position of agent to the local lord of the manor, Charles St George and whose flamboyant dress had impressed Kate's suitor Jack McCulloch. Victor de l'Herrault was a nervous man. Lauder, the other agent who was threatened, was a tougher character, well versed in the art of self-survival.

Both of the letters Michael preserved – one of them addressed to Lauder, the first to some unnamed colleague (perhaps himself?) – are headed with the outline of a coffin, surmounted with crossed bones, and the single word, 'deth'. Both are addressed from the 'Molly McGuires lodge' in an ill-educated script.

> take kare you do not get the sam tratement that i intind to give to Vicktor and lauder for i will shoot them both and you to if you do any thing that is not rite we will have no infernal frenchman in the place for he is a dam bad sort i warned Viktor and lauder i will not do it again sho this to them and mind yoursel

> Lauder you and Vicktor is having fine times do you think me or my childern are in the cuntry that you ar alloud to go on the way you ar eejectmint and notices. a man cant cut a tree but he must be find we will never be asy till you and Vicktor is shot now of the notices and eejectmints and put a stop to i have a good opertunity to shoot you both one of thes nites sho this to Vicktor i send him one this will be the last warning for i will shoot ye as i used dogs.

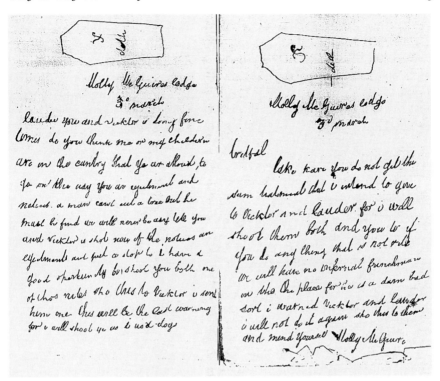

The two Molly McGuire letters.
(Courtesy of Trinity College Library, Manuscripts Room.)

Michael Mitchell kept a diary in 1854 and 1855 in which he recorded his daily activities in tiny script. He had been in the Provincial Bank for ten years at this date, and noted down the progress of his promotion and his pay from the beginning. The first year had been spent in his home town of Birr, after which he was transferred to Dungannon in Tyrone, at an annual salary of £40. His brother James had been nearby then, in Ballymena, doing well for himself, and soon promoted to accountant, but James soon left the Provincial, and eventually became manager of the Ulster Bank in Dublin.

Michael, still in the Provincial Bank, went to Ballina in February 1846, at a salary of £50. The following August he moved to Sligo, with an additional raise. His salary increased by leaps and bounds until in 1854 he was earning £120 a year and, when in November 1858 he was appointed manager of the newly opened branch in Carrick-on-Shannon, his earnings more than doubled, to £250.

The first entry, in the fly leaf of his diary, is a reminder of how vulnerable Sligo was to disease, as an international port of its day. Kate herself refers in her *Memoir* to her nurse, Mary Cleary, who remembered the 'First Cholera' in Sligo. Mary had been a young girl at the time, had visited a friend who had cholera, and told how she had drunk from a cup on the table beside the girl's bed, 'never taking the disease'. 'She used to say that there was a black cloud over the town at that time. Airley the Cooper, of Bridge Street, said that the town was so deserted during the epidemic that a footstep in Market Street could be heard quite plainly on the Mall.'

Michael, in more modern times, was equipped with a remedy which he wrote down:

Lump sugar ground	2ozs.
Prepared chalk	2ozs.
Ground ginger	1oz

Teaspoonfull to be taken every hour in a wine glass

½ & ½ full Brandy & Water

Said to be infallible

Or a mustard Emetic & after a glass of Brandy with a few grains of Cayenne pepper.

The Provincial Bank in Sligo was thriving in the 1850s when Michael was there. The first bank to open in the town, 30 years later it monopolised the major business of the county, as its arresting Renaissance-style facade, of Ballysodare limestone dressed with carved Mount Charles slabs, intimated importantly.

After a hard day's work, Michael's greatest pastime was walking, whether alone or in company. In winter, he dined after work, with his manager or with friends, after which he often slept. Then he played billiards or Loo – at which he frequently lost small sums of money. He 'saw girls'.

Too much enjoyment at the table quickly reaped its result. In November 1854, he was kept awake with a pain in his toe, which Dr Little confirmed as the beginning of gout. Heart and lungs were sound, though he was dyspeptic and appropriate tonics were ordered for his relief. He insured his life for £400.

His regular companion in Sligo was a man named McLeod, at whose house he slept sometimes after a dinner party, and who often came to breakfast at his lodgings. Another house he frequented was the Littles', for parties or cards, though he doesn't seem to have met Kate, another frequent visitor, at this period. However, he was inticed into her sister Bessie St Leger's social circle, and often dined at her house in the Mall, and played cards afterwards.

From April on, he often picnicked with friends on Lough Gill, and dined with the Gore-Booths at Lissadell or the Wynnes in their handsome Cassels designed house, Hazelwood. He swam. And he would walk alone in the demesne at Hazelwood, on the shores of Lough Gill. More frequently he walked alone in the woods, passing the shell house, the moss house and the rock house, looking at the long view of five or six miles of lake, the numberless islands. By the water's edge, an ageless liquid peace lapped against the rough stone moorings of the row boats, beneath silver barked trees thronged with song birds.

One duty, noted at the end of May 1854, was to travel to Dublin to collect bank notes and deliver a parcel to the Dublin office. He set out on a Wednesday morning at 8 o'clock, dined in Mullingar, and was in town at ten that night and, after delivering his parcel, slept at the Hibernian Hotel. In the morning, he walked to the Weggs for breakfast (his sister Susan had married a Colonel Wegg much older than herself), he had a leisurely conversation, and then went to the office in William Street. Work completed, he went for a drive with a friend, and returned to Susan for dinner. In the evening he attended a meeting of the Masonic Grand Lodge, with time to go to the theatre afterwards.

Carrying 'a large amount of notes' to the coach in the morning, he was feeling extremely unwell – perhaps from too much port at the Grand Lodge! – but a Miss Duncan on the coach was attentive, and he arrived safely in Sligo at 9 o'clock on Friday night, visited the manager of the bank to relieve himself of his precious bundle, and then headed home.

His 1855 diary outlines the same pattern of life with a lot of walking, at Hazelwood, about the Strand or Rosses Point, Coney Island, Lissadell and up the Lake. He was meeting the St Legers or visiting them regularly, winning or losing at Loo; and, by October, some of the Cullens had joined the party, playing cards at the St Legers' house or at the Littles. Inevitably there were evenings of singing, which he enjoyed. But he doesn't mention Kate Cullen, and would surely have remembered her rich contralto, accompanied by Dr Little as countertenor in their soulful duets, if she had been there when he was.

The rather too sumptuous round of pleasure continued. The bill of fare for the Grand Jury Summer Assizes Dinner of 1856 – he presumably acted as Accountant to the Grand Jury – gives an idea of the kind of indulgence that was to hasten his premature demise.

GRAND JURY, SUMMER ASSIZES, 1856.
BILL OF FARE

| | | Cuiseniere, |
| July 14th. | | MRS HALL, Court-House. |

First Course	Turbot removed by	
	Saddle of Mutton	
Fricondeau of Veal		Lamb Cutlets
Tomato Sauce		Cucumber Sauce

| Roast Ducks | | Tongue with stewed Endive |

| Croquets a la Reine | | Lobster Paties |
| Soup a la Printainiere | | Mock Turtle Soup |

| Removed by Ham | | Removed by braized |
| and Spinach | | Fillit of Veal |

| Chicken Paties | | Sweetbreads, Larded, |
| | | and Mushroom. |

| Raised Pie, a la Perigord | | Boiled Fowls Bechemel |
| | | Sauce |

| Lamb Cutlets | | Fillits of Mutton, |
| Tarragon Sauce | | A la Soubice |

Salmon removed by
A Roast Sirloin of Beef

Second Course	Turkey Polts,	
	Removed by Plum Pudding.	
Curacoe Jelly		Vanilla Cream

| Charlotte Russe | | Maringle |

| French Pastry | | Rutland Puffs |

| Mayonaise of Chicken | | Lobster Salad |
| Gateau a la Reine | | French Pastry |

| Almond Cheesecakes | | Raspberry Tartlets |

| Lemon Cream | | Wine Jelly |

Ducklings removed by
Plum Pudding[2]

---

2.   Menu found among Michael Mitchell's papers.

With broading waistline, Michael took exercise at balls everywhere in the province, going as far as Ballina, in County Mayo, on more than one occasion, where, after a 'very pleasant party till ½ past 3, we started for Sligo'. He fished up the Lough, he caught pike, afterwards dancing some more. There were moments of depression, as when he lost £25 cash at the bank, and did not get to bed until two o'clock as a result. He was conscientious, and drew a bill to cover the loss.

Social pleasures apart, Michael Mitchell was a serious young man and to one aspect of his life he attached great importance, his membership of the Masonic Order. He had been initiated into Lodge 20 in Sligo, in September 1850, and had been elevated to Fellowcraft degree on his second night when, the following month, on October 3, he was admitted as a Master Mason. In July 1851, he was raised to Mark Master Mason's Degree, and exalted as a Royal Arch Mason, after which, in August, he was admitted to the mysteries of the Lodge Chapter. October 1852 saw him knighted as a Knight Templar and six months later he was made a Knight of the Sword, Knight of the East, and Knight of the East and West in St John's Lodge. Not long afterwards, he was elected Secretary of the Lodge.

All of the ceremonial, and the successive honours, made an enormous impression on him, noted down in his pleasant free flowing script, together with the names of those who conferred the honours, as well as details of the new brethren he himself conducted through their degrees.[3]

On his appointment to the bank in Carrick-on-Shannon in 1858, he made friends at once with the local landlord, Charles Manners St George, and had as a constant companion St George's French aide, Victor de l'Herrault. One of the first obligations of his office was to act as patron for the Court house performance of

The great Drama of thrilling interest,

Entitled 'Valsha: the Slave Queen and Victim!

in which local amateurs joined travelling players to form a melodramatic cast.

Inevitably, Michael was drawn to Shannon Lodge, as Jack McCulloch and James Long had been ten years before. Diana Faris's late husband Alick had been a Brother Mason and, armed with an introduction from Bessy St

---

3.   When he moved to Carrick-on-Shannon in November 1858, he joined Lodge no. 854 and his Brothers regarded the period after he joined, the early sixties, as the most flourishing period of its history, 'due, no doubt, to the great Masonic learning, ability and zeal, of our distinguished Brother Mitchell'. Records of *'Concord Lodge', 1797-1897*, p. 16. See also p. 93, note 5.

Leger in Sligo, he soon found that he could not resist the Cullen warmth of the widow (Kate's sister). As for Diana, Michael fitted instantly into the social circle. Was he not the new acquaintance of her secret admirer, Victor de l'Herrault?

Just a year after his arrival in Carrick, Michael heard Kate Cullen singing at a charity concert. Her sister Diana introduced them afterwards and the bank manager was immediately in pursuit – with the excuse of contributing to a worthy charity!

> My dear Miss Kate,
>
> The Cause must be a good one when the pleader is eminently so, and the enclosed card represents my own name for a Crown – being the head of the Establishment – and the Accountant for one shilling, which he hopes you will not refuse from the gentleman who wore the very white hat, and admired the sweetness of your voice so much the evening you arrived in this simple village. . . .

The approach had been made. The young man's bantering intellectual tone evidently appealed, and, before many months had elapsed, during a hasty visit to Sligo on a Sunday afternoon in January, he made plain his intentions, and returned to Carrick a happy man.

The experienced Victor had acted as go-between at a crucial stage of the courtship. Michael, dazed, but not too much to write a short note immediately on his return to his betrothed (hoping that he would make himself worthy of her), was concerned that poor Victor, eating out his heart for Kate's sister, Diana, must stand by and watch him at the summit of his happiness.

10

Love's Self

Carrick-on-Shannon 1860

Michael wrote formally to his betrothed the following day, calling her 'Kate' instead of using her pet name 'Kitzy'. He was in a responsible mood, revealing his spiritual side alongside the practicality that was innate in the Mitchells. He sent her a tablet that had belonged to his late sister Sarah, 'who found a Saviour in the Lord Jesus, who loved me dearly, and whose letters breathed forth a pure and peaceful love'.

The immediate matter was the bank house. He wrote at once to London for leave to send in an estimate for painting and papering. He would consult Brother St Leger about getting furniture for the drawing-room. Mrs Faris, who was on the spot, would give him a helping hand with carpets and curtains.

Michael Mitchell's envelopes were fastened down with various seals, one representing an archangel, with the gothic initials 'M.M.' beneath it. An embossed archangel also appeared on the flap of the envelope, and sometimes on his writing paper – the same Archangel Michael who gave the family his name and surmounted the family crest. The motto, 'Sapiens qui Assiduus', was appropriate for the hardworking Mitchells.

Michael Thomas Mitchell's bookplate with Mitchell coat-of-arms.
Private collection, Dublin.

Substantial Michael was proud of his connection with the insubstantial. Despite his low opinion of his own spiritual worth – one wonders what exactly was the depth of his depravity, and was it more culpable than the tendency to self-indulgence – he valued his relationship with the highest of the angels. He discussed with Kate as to whether she would prefer an unsilvered angel on her envelopes, and how many should be ordered and samples were sent from Waller's in Dublin.

He wanted Kate to choose for herself how she would address him. 'Call me Mickey,' he wrote on the fifth day of their engagement.

> It is not too free. – Or by the name of the Archangel, whence our family Sir-name is derived, though perhaps you would not like yet to set me up amongst the Hierarchy – until you see whether or not I am your good Angel, which God grant I may be, as you are and will be mine, I feel full well. Do you know your own name in the Greek signifies *Purity?*

Already Carrick-on-Shannon was abrim with gossip, and he wrote with relish,

> I heard today I was married to Mrs Faris on Monday morning, quick work!! Well, be it so. She can allow it so, and keep our secret quiet a little longer. Let it come out gradually. . . . To tell you the truth, Kitzy, I would have made love to you long since more openly, only I could not see my way; and if I had been successful the delay would have caused enough of gossip – never mind – let them talk away as you say. – I would be delighted they knew my good luck, but as you wish to keep it quiet let it be so.

Michael was always inventing appropriate nicknames for his friends and acquaintances. One frequent visitor at his house, 'the Conqueror', was probably the agent, William Lauder. Diana Faris was always 'the Widow'. Then there was 'the Duchess'; and the St Legers were the 'King' and 'Queen' living at 'the Palace'. He told Kate that he would amuse himself foiling the personal questions fired at him by the colleague he named 'Pickwick', who would be pumping him.

Michael approved of her mother, and of Janey and James, and sent them his love. His own old mother, Susan Langstaff, frail but interminable, was delighted he was to settle down. His sister Margaret had been praying God would send him the wife Kate sounded to be from her description. Thomas, the crusty bachelor, who had met Mrs St Leger and Mrs Faris 'and admired the former amazingly', wished he had seen Kate first.

> My brother Adam, who is really the Moon & Sun of good nature, says he heard it – he writes to me himself – congratulatory. . . .

Then sister Susan Wegg, whose special pet Michael had been as a child, wrote complimenting him from Parsonstown, where she and her husband, the Colonel – 'a queer fish, but a right good fellow' – had been spending Christmas.

He had a good story to tell about the way gossip burgeoned in Carrick. There had been a bonfire to celebrate Mrs Peyton's return to Castlecarrow – 'poor Woman, I dont suppose she is much improved'.

> They then returned, some of James's Company of Royal Rifles, and came with a fiddler to Shannon Lodge, where they danced in the Porch and Mr Mullany, I think, a Rifle Man, addressed the audience, having drawn them up in files at either side of the door, and what do you think he said? '3 Cheers for Mr & Mrs Victor.' The Widow loked queer when I told her this, as she and Victor went upstairs to see them out of the window overhead. Victor would not come down so I had to go to the Door and present the ruffians with my two good looking half crowns and then they gave long loud and lusty cheers all the way down the Avenue for Mr Mitchell, and long may he reign in Carrick over the National Bank. I thought they would have cheered for Mrs Mitchell, but they forgot that part.

Obviously Carrick-on-Shannon was in total confusion about the lot of them – the Widow Faris, Monsieur de l'Herrault and Mr Mitchell – never mind what bank he was at. Michael had even been told by one party that his wedding day was to be March 1st – 'I still look unconscious.'

Michael was religious, but he was not pious, and he sometimes got into trouble with his bride-to-be. One Sunday in Sligo he attended the Congregational Church with Kate, and Janey – a quiet devout spinster in her late thirties, much loved by the family – and he made an unforgivable faux-pas. He had fallen asleep during the sermon and that had not been all!

> Do forgive me if I said anything that would have annoyed you or Janey about the 'Preacher'. The fact is, an unaccountable heaviness came over me during part of the sermon, something like Adam's deep sleep, and lo! I found you beside me, my future rib. It was a pleasant dream really, I could not control it, but I often say things about preachers, etc., that are not meant for more than to see what opinion others have of them. I recollect when first I heard Guinness [the renowned preacher of the day] I was not inclined to like him, and threw out hints against him, and when I heard replies it made me think about him more and like him better.

Peace was made with both women, but there would always be a slight friction between himself and Kate when they married, because he was ortho-

dox in worship, valuing spiritual symbols, looking for metaphorical analogies
(traits his poet daughter Susan inherited); while Kate was drawn more and
more to the fundamentalists, and particularly the Congregational Church. He
was sympathetic, and prepared to be tactful:

> You are quite right that I prefer our own dear Church of England to any
> Conventicle,[1] and its liturgy to any prayers that I have ever heard ut-
> tered by mortals. They are the best, I am persuaded, however that will
> not make me love the less my dear child, who does like those places, for
> I know what's Hallowed Ground. . . . I love the ancient orders, as I
> belong to one myself, and the solemn Temples, being a Templar – still
> I can quote for your satisfaction what is really hallowed ground – pure
> affection, sincere devotion and holy love in man's heart, and directing
> his thought to the great 'I am' for health and succour, faith and hope,
> whether on the mountain top, in the closet or the Church.

Kate, with her low church leaning, tended to take matters of faith liter-
ally and the unfortunate man frequently found himself speaking out of turn.
They had a serious debacle during one of his visits to Sligo, when she accused
him of insinuating that she was a swaddler[2] – the current nickname for a
Methodist – and left the dinner table in a fury.

Michael, under the blackest of clouds, wrote to her after the weekend
with his usual reasonableness:

> I remember when the King spoke to me about your going to meetings
> &c on the first day, that I said I respected your prejudices, and that I
> would not interfere with them. I believe, myself, that it never gave me
> any uneasiness, the thought of your having peculiar religious views, and
> far be it from me, my dearest Kate, to apply the epithet of Swaddler to
> you. I durst not do it, I could not, for I could not for one moment
> suppose you are such a one as I could apply that name to. . . . I know
> many in Sligo who are, but for my definition of it I must tell you
> another time, it may not be the same as yours. I do not apply it to all
> who go away from our own Church and seek the means of grace in other
> congregations or who by their life and conversation seek to adorn the
> Doctrine of God their Saviour in all things. No, no, the reverse. I
> confine it to some vaniglorious [sic] few who make religion a Cloak to
> work out ends that are not compatible with its tenets or margins, and

---

1.   Meetings of non-conformists, viewed with suspicion by authorities of the Established
     Church. Referring to his Church as the 'Church of England', Michael uses an abbreviated
     form of the name (The United Church of England and Ireland) by which the Church of
     Ireland was known from the time of the Act of Union until Disestablishment in 1870.
2.   Joyce, in 'An Encounter' in *Dubliners*, uses 'swaddlers' as a general term for Protestants.

who wish to appear in churches for the purpose of being heard and Seen.

He urged her to adopt a wider, calmer approach to religion and the Archangel's injured, placatory tones quickly brought about a reconciliation.

Michael wrote all of his love letters to Kate on Provincial Bank of Ireland paper, a small blue page, with a shiny surface, but he made no apology, because he said he was so used to writing on it that he preferred it to any other. Once he seized up a page at the office, before walking down to Shannon Lodge and dinner with Victor, and pencilled a rapid note simply to tell her about a fresh spring walk near Killukin.

Kate still longed for a secret wedding and Michael proposed one solution. Victor must be kept out of it, though he would be disappointed at not being prime mover, as he had been so useful during the early days of their courtship. The secret of the wedding day must be kept to themselves 'and Royalty' (the St Legers).

> A funny thing strikes me. Were I to go down of a Saturday night as I hope please God to do tomorrow, remain in Sligo on Sunday, return here on Sunday night just having got as many friends as I could to accompany me to the Coach, and chat and make public my departure. Come back by the mail on Monday morning reaching Sligo at 7 o'c and letting no one know my movements but Pickwick, who would gladly join and disappoint the people; and with him by my side and your little self all ready, we could nicely manage to give the people the go by – no talk of carriage to go away at all until all was over.

These private discussions absorbed them happily. For the moment, he told her, he would be coming down with a sample of wedding ring and guard, to try for size, and with carpet patterns, which, he hoped, would arrive in time by boat. 'If so, I shall be a regular bag man[3] with nine samples.' He had two brace of snipe for the King – 'His Majesty likes game, I think'. (He was constantly supplying the St Legers with hare, widgeon or game birds, though he was not a sportsman himself.) The weekend was a great success, and he came back to Carrick in sublimate mood, bringing with him Sligo oysters to feed the Conqueror.

Even in his lonely state, he did not forget to apply himself to practical matters. He had one faithful man servant, John, and had otherwise depended on part-time labour in the house. But now he engaged a new cook-and-housemaid, whom he hoped would prove satisfactory when Kate came to live in the bank house. For the next few weeks his comments were constantly

---

3.   A commercial traveller.

about servants, interspersed with complaints about Victor, who was staying with him.

> I will not have an old woman again for love or money. They always scheme, and drink tea. A young one is far better. Old ones grumble about trifles, and young ones are more anxious to do what they are desired. . . . I thought I had a treasure for you in old Honor Mills, indeed I would have been as well satisfied had I kept Rose, notwithstanding her lachrymose appearance: but Mrs Faris persuaded me to part with her for Honor, and Victor also put in a stave.

> So much for allowing other people to meddle in one's domestic affairs. Believe me I will eschew such interference again, as for the last week, my servant John, with the assistance of a slave has been doing the duties of cook and Housemaid and above all attending Victor, who requires his boots laced, his leggings buttoned, hot water baths and cold water baths, in fact I do not trouble the man to do much for me he is so taken up with the distinguished foreigner, who, I must assure you, in confidence, is a great nuisance. I hate an idle body. I thought he would have gone away yesterday but he finds his quarters too pleasant.

In fact Michael forgot that he would have no old woman again, and laughed to Kate about his new housekeeper, who was a character:

> Mrs Robinson is a most bustling old Woman. . . . Her dialect has been formed by mixing high Dutch and low Dutch, Irish & English and Cork & channel fleet jargons together. She is very funny looking and what with Clarcal [clerical] meetings, her dather [daughter], stuffing up Mr Hamilton's plate in the Chimneys for fear of Robbers . . . she has got enough to say.

Mrs Robinson joked away with the workmen decorating the house, 'and appears as brisk as a fairy'. So brisk was she, that she was scouring the rooms before they were finished, despite her sore eye. No one could stop her. 'She is a perfect Majoress Domo'. Only John, his man was rather huffed, and disgusted that with all the cleaning operations the bank manager had to dine in his little office.

Though as a carefree bachelor he had found Victor's company entertaining, Michael, like Kate, was now irritated with his friend. However, he counselled Kate to 'make allowances for people in love.' Diana was bewildered, but continued to adore Victor, despite the fact that he was difficult. He was such a hypochondriac that he had told Sydney Kirkwood that the date of his own wedding would depend on the state of his health.

Michael gave Kate an example of how the Frenchman magnified his indispositions:

Victor has just been ill. Why? he had a *little* soup, a *very small* bit of mutton chop, a *tiny* bit of Oswego, a glass of sherry on top of that, and a glass to drink after, and then only *Half* a glass of grog. This for his Lunch. He then came down town in the Conqueror's Coat. Walked back to Shannon Lodge and felt quite faint from walking so heavily clad, the coat being 1/2 hundred weight, and enough to worry a man as strong again, or perhaps he laughed too much with Coote Hutchinson, but so it was, poor fellow. I left him reclining on the sofa and drinking a *very little bit* of Oswego to restore him again.

On March 12, Michael had news from the Directors about his leave, but wrote to Kate rather shaken, and relieved to have escaped unscathed from an accident, on the road home from Sligo.

The horses, leaders, took fright, after leaving Boyle and rushed at a wall on the Roadside and very nearly upset the Coach. I did not see the danger until it was over. Had there been a precipice undefended, in all probablity we would have come to grief. . . .

They were certain, after suggestions of Dromahaire, Dublin and Donegal, that they wanted to marry in Sligo, taking the St Legers into their confidence, but no one else. The Conqueror, Lauder, who was now renting Shannon Lodge, offered his horses for the occasion. In Sligo, rumour still had it that they would go to Donegal to be married by Labatt.

Kate attended auctions with Bessie looking for furniture – giving the Queen her head in so far as she and Michael allowed. 'I think what you say about dressing tables in *petticoats* a very nice arrangement;' was Michael's comment. 'Indeed now that I think of it it is a most proper one.' She would also be responsible for the drawing-room papers, and for the paper in their bedroom. Michael would choose the parlour paper, but he was worried about painting the drawing-room ceiling in oil. This was not in the estimate, and he did not wish the painter to lose even one shilling in the transaction. 'He is a Brother Mason above all things, but he is a fellow man too.'

Michael filled his frequent letters to Kitzy with sentimental, religious and poetic passages. On April 1, he was revelling in the promises of Spring:

The Bleakest rock upon the basement heath
Feels in its loneliness some touch of Spring,

he wrote, enclosing some scented white violets, which he had pulled at Shannon Lodge. Walking, he became eloquent.

There is something really beautiful in the return of Spring, a fresh existence, a new moving power, a never ending, always returning, verdure, a thought of the immortal, Eternal beauty, that shall reign when we are glorified and walk the earth again clothed in the white Robes.

On April 9, he was writing to her about very different weather.

The Elements generally do battle against your devoted lover's advent to Sligo, and furiously fret and rage after him on his return to his quiet domicile, it needs all the Soothing influence of my beloved to soften down the effects of their wild war on my frame, and requires my own cool philosophy, on my return, to tell me they are rapidly blowing away my dusty old Bachelorhood. So your angel settles his pinions and Stands quietly to order, ready again and yet again, perhaps, to fly forth and come back with the dove, his love.

It had hailed, and snowed, and blown on his way back to Carrick, but he was lucky enough to find a seat inside the Royal Mail coach, which plied twice daily between Dublin, Carrick, Boyle and Sligo, in the company of a young gentleman and Mr Gulley, who had a caged thrush he was taking as a present to a friend.

Belatedly and apologetically, he was arranging with Pollocks in Dublin for the settlement of Kate's own money on herself; including in the arrangement the insurance he had for £400, which he hoped to increase with either an additional £600, or by allotting £40 a year out of his income. This was a matter much on his conscience which he should have discussed with her mother when in Sligo.

Their marriage plans were completed on April 17, when Michael heard from his deputy Cooper that he could definitely be in Carrick on the 23rd or 24th to take over the bank for the interim; and that Michael would be free on the 25th. After Cooper's arrival on the 24th, Michael wrote to Kate from the bank house in fervent mood:

My dearest Kate, I can only say now, and perhaps these are the last lines that I shall ever pen to you other than as your husband – that no matter how Providence may bless my course, no matter what prospects are before me . . . I have an Earnest desire to your temporal . . . a thoughtful prayer for your Eternal welfare. I can say no more. If I have made any false professions do not hesitate to tell me so, but if I act up to them, my dearest, oh come along and we shall indeed be one. We shall, we shall. . . .

11

Love's Heavenly Face

Sligo and Carrick-on-Shannon 1860-64

Kate and Michael succeeded in having a quiet wedding. Michael didn't anticipate as much publicity as Kate did, though he admitted he disliked being the centre of attention, and was particularly nervous and shaky at the thought of the people of the Mall staring on that eventful morning. Kate says little about the marriage in her *Memoir*, but she was self-conscious about her age.

'My wedding was a private one, and very quiet', she recounts. It took place on 26 April, 1860, in Calry Church – the church the St Legers attended. A plain, Gothic-style building erected about the time Noblett had come to Sligo, with simple castellation and decorative pinnacles, it projects breadth and assurance rather than elegance, but was certainly the fashionable place to be married. Edward Labatt, with the Rector, performed the ceremony. Kate wore a grey silk dress and white bonnet and tulle veil and orange blossoms – 'being considered too old to wear white!' Her sister Janey was bridesmaid, and Michael's colleague, Richard Gordon, was best man. None of Michael's family was there, as he had explained to them that he wanted 'no gathering of the clans'. After the wedding, the small party went to the St Leger's house nearby for a déjeuner, the wedding cake baked by Bessie.

The couple went to Edinburgh for their wedding tour, where they stayed for a few days at the Caledonian Hotel, and then, Kate recalled,

> travelled through the Highlands, and saw Holyrood, and the lakes, the Trossacks, in fact everything that was to be seen, and which every unfortunate bride and bridegroom have to inspect. . . .

> heard Dr Guthrie preach a very fine sermon in Edinburgh. One Saturday night was spent looking at a very good picture-gallery. We were in Scotland about ten days, stayed also in Birr for some days with my husband's people and then came home to our house in Carrick. There I began my married life, and received and had to return a great number of visits.

Kate knew Carrick-on-Shannon already from childhood and her prolonged visits to her sister at Shannon Lodge. As the chief market for grain and provisions in County Leitrim, it had been little more than one main street, unpaved and imperfectly lit, until Charles Manners St George the landlord, a much travelled diplomat, had improved it, building the market square in 1839, erecting a market house and shambles. The court house, like many in provincial Ireland, was elegant, with a facade of four Doric columns and here, besides the assizes, various entertainments and meetings – including the Masonic dinners, took place. Kate herself, as we have seen, had sung there.

When the Provincial Bank opened in Carrick in 1858, a house in Main Street[1] was leased at £40 a year from St George. Michael, the first manager, and his bride lived over the bank premises. It was quite different from the grandiloquent building in Sligo, being a simple country town house converted into an office. Carrick's two hotels were in the same street, one opposite, one beside the bank. Church's, the superior one, known once as the St George's Arms, was the posting-house, and had acted as agent for the National Bank before the Provincial Bank opened.

Kate remembered that 'every Saturday the shopkeepers entrusted their money to 'Jemmy Church' to lodge in the National Bank in Boyle. . . . Every Monday Jemmy again appeared, and conveyed the money necessary for the week's use back to Carrick, where it went through the same process again at the end of the week.

> Jemmy Church was . . . a singularly honest man, and conveyed everyone's money backwards and forwards without loss of a penny, and I never heard that anyone attempted to rob him. At the same time he was considered to be only half-witted. He wore a long black coat, white corduroy trousers, good shoes (provided by the Lord of the Soil, Mr St George) and stockings and a tall hat. He had black hair and had a ferocious look. He carried a thick white stick and always kept a bundle of pieces of glass in his hand for the purpose of scraping it white. His pockets were always bulging with newspapers. His name was not really 'Church', but as he had been the messenger of the Church family for years, the name of 'Church' stuck to him for life. He had been a great drunkard in his early days, but took the pledge from Father Mathew, and kept it ever afterwards.

Another man she remembered was 'The Drummy', who went for messages, and watered the horses for the Bianconi cars and coaches in Church's yard.[2] McCloskey, the guard on the day coach from Sligo, wore a frock coat and cap, and had a humorous tongue. He was so well read that he was

---

1.   Now Bridge Street.
2.   Kate in her *Memoir* states 'The horses for the coach were kept at Church's Hotel. They were owned by Bianconi . . . the famous Italian who introduced the "Bianconi (long) cars", which are still used in some parts of the country (or were a few years ago). He also ran

reputed to have had a college education, and some said he was a spoiled priest.

> We used to think it great fun to travel outside to hear him talk. He was especially attentive to young ladies travelling by themselves, who were always given into his charge. He remained on the coaches till trains came in, when he took his place as guard of the train. 'Well, McCloskey', said Madame de l'Herrault, 'so you left the coach!' 'No, Ma'am,' replied McCloskey, 'but the coach left me'!

> An Englishman travelling once by the coach fell into conversation with McCloskey and the subject of pets was discussed. 'Well now', said McC., 'I have a very curious pet: I suppose you never heard of such a pet.' 'What is that', said the Englishman. 'Well,' said McC., 'it's a pet lobster.' The Englishman finding it hard to believe this, McC said, 'Well now, if you come out to my house at Sandymount this evening, I'll show him to you.

> The Englishman accepted the invitation joyfully and McC brought him out to his house on their arrival in Dublin. McC., on entering the house, said to his wife, 'Where's Roger?' 'Roger', said she, looking round the room, 'oh he's gone out for a walk on the Strand'. 'I'm afraid in that case,' said McC., turning to the Englishman, 'I won't be able to show him to you this evening, for when he goes out there he never knows when to come back!'

'The Englishman', Kate adds, 'on his return to his native island, no doubt retailed this story as an instance of the strange customs of the Irish.'[3]

Romance was still an engrossing preoccupation, though Michael and Kate could now sit back and observe the intrigues of others. Victor and Diana were still unresolved about their topsy-turvy relationship. Shortly after his engagement, Michael had been writing to Kate asking, 'Is Victor coming really round. He is slow about it.'

---

coaches all over the country. He kept splendid horses for both coaches and cars, his system continued till trains took possession of the field. Of course there were no trains in my early days. My first journey to Dublin from Leitrim was by coach'. The railway was opened towards the end of 1862, and Michael Mitchell makes reference to it in a letter of 4 October of that year.

3. Trollope in his first novel, *The Macdermotts of Ballycloren* (1847), says he learned the story of Ballycloren from his friend McCloskey, 'Mc—— who knows everything . . . and, reader, if I thought it would ever be your good fortune to hear the history of Ballycloran from the guard of the Boyle coach, I would recommend you to get it from him, and shut my book forthwith' (*The Macdermotts of Ballycloran* with an introduction by R. L. Wolff, 1979, vol. 1, pp. 10-11). It is tempting to contemplate that he may have been the Englishman mentioned in Kate's anecdote.

No one really knew where Victor Levy de l'Herrault came from. Charles Manners St George, and his Swedish wife, had taken a fancy to him, when they met him, travelling in Italy, in great grief after the death of his mother. This was in 1847. They invited him back to Carrick to Hatley Manor, where they spent a good part of each year, waking up the neighbourhood with their entertaining. Victor remained on at Hatley to manage their affairs. The mystery as to his origins was never fully resolved. 'Some called him handsome. He had fine eyes, which were his best feature, good teeth, and looked well when in full evening dress. He was a man of medium height', according to Kate.

The first time Kate had seen him at Hatley Manor, he wore a brown cloth coat with gilt buttons and a black tie with a crimson bow attached.

> His English at this time was very broken but it improved greatly, and he could afterwards speak it very passably. He... sang well both Italian and French songs . . . his voice was one of the sweetest tenors I ever heard and of very good volume. He was a good linguist, and some people considered that Italian must be his native language he spoke it so well.

Hatley Manor, Carrick-on-Shannon, residence of Charles Manners St. George.
(Photograph courtesy of Shane Flynn.)

. . . I think he admired my sister from the moment he saw her. She was certainly very handsome, very like my father, whose appearance always created a sensation whatever place he entered.

While Kate and Michael were still deciding their wedding plans, Diana and Victor had left Carrick separately, Diana travelling to Dublin, Victor to London, and they met together in Italy where they toured with the St Georges, and Diana's sister-in-law, Sara Faris. Away from Carrick, in the congenial company of the St Georges, the couple quickly made up their minds.

Diana wrote to Kate from Genoa on August 7:

> We find that to be married here would be attended with a good deal of trouble and delay, especially as we both belong to different nations. And, under any circumstance, we should have to be married over again in either England or Ireland to make it legal. . . . We have come to the conclusion to enjoy this place (of which I should never be tired) and to go back to get married either in England or Ireland. Victor is most anxious to get all over quickly so we will return to England in a short time. Both Mr and Mrs St George highly approve of this plan although they regret his departure. . . .

The small Irish party drove through Sestri, Corrigliano & Peglea ('where Christopher Columbus disembarked to enable his entrée into Genoa after discovering America'), Diana amazed at the contrast between the plain exteriors and the rich interiors of the baroque Chapels they examined. They went to the opera, and a comedy, and an amateur performance for the benefit of the Sicilian insurrection, 'crowded with Garabaldinis'.

In August 1860, on their way back through London, Victor and Diana were married, with Colonel Faris of the Royal Engineers, Diana's brother-in-law, giving her away, and Sara Faris, the Colonel's sister, acting as a witness.

On their return to Carrick, the de l'Herraults lived at Hatley Manor, Shannon Lodge having been rented to William Lauder. It was an unsatisfactory match. Victor, despite his undeniable charm, at last revealed how unbalanced his temperament was. He was suspicious of gossip in Carrick society, uneasy about his standing there. Matters reached a high pitch in April 1868. He sent Michael copies in French and English of letters he had received from the St Georges in May 1847 when they were living at the Villa d'Elci in Florence, and had persuaded him to travel with them on a visit to England and Ireland. 'Il vaut la Peine de voir ces deux Pays,' wrote St George, 'dont l'un est Prospere Peutetre au dela de tout Example, & l'autre dans un État de transition tres interessante.'[4]

---

4. 'It is worth seeing these two countries of which one is prosperous – perhaps more than any other – and the other in a very interesting state of transition.'

Victor said he had first met the St Georges in the late spring of 1847, in the foyer of a hotel in the Piazza della Erimita in Florence. They had taken to each other at once, Victor discussing politics with Charles, and finding they shared views on the Whigs – 'the Horrors' – and on government ministry generally, and the plight of the poorer classes. Christina St George succumbed readily to his affectionate ways with her turtles, and her little dog, Jack. So they wrote to him later, when he was at Turin, to renew their invitation to travel back with them to Ireland.

Now, 20 years later, Victor feared that 'blaguard' reports about his association with the St Georges were about to 'ooze out', and he was sending Michael these letters as proof about the warmth and authenticity of their friendship, so that any gossip might be contradicted.[5] His anxiety was probably quite unnecessary, but was symptomatic of his mental state. 'He began to show signs of insanity', remarks Kate in her memoir, 'and eventually had to be placed in an Asylum in Dublin, where he died in 1869.' Diana survived him by 20 years. First she went to live in Sligo, with Bessie St Leger, letting her house, Shannon Lodge, to her brother Jemmy and later she returned to Shannon Lodge, where she died in 1890.

If Diana's love affair was long drawn out and painful, marred first by the presence of an ageing husband, and then, when she was free, by the intransigence of her lover, the other members of her family conducted their affairs of the heart with less outward flourish. Michael was trying to detect Jemmy's feelings about a certain widow in Carrick. 'He is, I think, beginning to simmer. I may make him boil . . .' he claimed.

Even more tantalising to the patient observer was the tender devotion that sober Janey (who had presided at tea in the schoolroom at Skreeney), Kate's senior by eight years, had for a certain clergyman in Sligo, a cleric so fascinating that he had lured Kate to conventicles on some of the precious evenings Michael had been able to snatch at Sligo during the days of their engagement. Kate, as the more outgoing of the two sisters, may have been acting unconsciously as ambassador in the secret affair. Certainly she would have been sympathetic to Janey's secret and hopeless, yet determined, love.

The Reverend Noble Shepperd had been Minister of the Independent Chapel in Newry for half-a-dozen years before coming to the congregation in Sligo in 1835 – where he was to remain for the rest of his life. Sligo's Independent Church owed its existence to a Scottish Presbyterian, who preceded Shepperd. The members met regularly in Waste Garden Lane, until, principally through preaching tours in Scotland and England, Shepperd had raised the sum of £3000 in order to build a permanent Church with manse

---

5.   It may be that it was at this juncture that Michael acquired the Molly Maguire letters, see
     p. 85.

and school, in 1850, in Stephen Street. He was a friend of Henry Grattan Guinness, the popular and dynamic preacher of the time, who when conducting a mission in the five principal towns of Ireland in 1859 – Cork, Limerick, Derry, Belfast and Dublin – had paid a flying visit to Sligo to see Noble Shepperd.

Janey was stirred by Shepperd's total and inspired dedication to his calling. Nearly 60, Noble Shepperd was still sprightly, and commandingly handsome. She attended every Sunday service without fail, as well as all his bible study meetings, and the lectures on Mondays and Wednesdays.

Moving with Jemmy, after Bidz's death, to live with the Mitchells in Carrick, gave Janey the opportunity to correspond with Shepperd's invalid wife, and with Shepperd himself, to whom she reported the 'miserable moral condition' that prevailed in Carrick. He was genial in his reply, but tactful. He missed her at Sunday worship, and at the lectures; and told her that if it were possible to get a public room in Carrick, he would be willing to go up and preach occasionally – 'especially if I knew there were a few beside yourself who sighed and cried over the miserable moral condition you describe.'

Mrs Shepperd, ailing and elderly, was visiting Bundoran, to take beneficial warm baths, and was touched by the enquiries of her 'kindliest' friend, Janey Cullen.

In March 1864, Mrs Shepperd's illness had reached a critical point. She had two nurses, then three, and as pain increased, she complained the less. She 'apologises for the occasional groan which is forced from her – she and we must now wait to see what the Lord means to do.' The Lord did not delay. Four more weeks of suffering, and Noble's wife passed away. 'I am just a big old Child,' Noble wrote to Janey in grief and confusion, 'and her who was all to me is left me for a little.'

Not for nothing had Janey earned the family nickname, 'Janey go-for-it'.[6] She wasn't the only woman in the congregation who had an interest in Noble Shepperd and he was now alone in his manse. He prided himself on his excellent health, and gained consolation from addressing himself with fresh vigour to his public duties. When he went to preach in Derry, she invited him to Carrick – but he went home by Enniskillen. When she holidayed with Kate at Rosses Point in July, he excused himself from not spending a day with them.

However, he was evidently weakening. Writing to Rosses Point, he suggested that he might come down one evening. 'I will just run down without notice and surprise you. I shall risk your not being at home, you are not likely to be far off.' 'I am afraid to indulge the hope of your being up on Sunday', he said, 'The weather is so warm.'

---

6.   Susan L. Mitchell (Kate's daughter) to her niece, Marjorie Brabazon, 6 February, 1923.

The evening at Rosses Point, so casually arranged, must have been a success, though there is no record of what happened. But Janey's hopes were advanced. Noble went to London later in the month, and, on his return through Dublin on August 3, sat down to write, not to Miss Cullen, but to 'My dear Jeany'. He had had the unusual treat in London of hearing three sermons on Sunday. Monday was spent at the Museum and the Zoological Gardens. He had left the previous morning, and reached Dublin, after a smooth passage, in the evening.

Despite the glorious weather, Janey was not to be dissuaded from coming up from the Point each Sunday, to be as near Noble as either of them dared during the service, and of course to hear the beautiful sermon of a visiting preacher. She and Kate extended their holiday in Sligo. Noble's replies to her constant bombarding courtship are written on mourning paper, with its broad black edge. He showed little resistance. On August 30, he apologised for not answering her 'unmistakeable love letter' at once.

> If I don't love you warmly, dearest Janey, I shall be very ungrateful, for your affection seems unbounded. I am not going to scold you for it however. I am afraid I like it too well and enjoy it too much.

She had made her conquest.

The family did not take to the affair at all eagerly. They were surprised and embarrassed. Janey at 40 should have resigned herself to spinsterhood. As soon as they suspected a serious engagement, they were warning Noble of the consequences. Noble pleaded with her to stay on good terms with the family, to seize any opportunity to improve relations. He thought, with such dissimilarity of tastes and habits, they were unlikely to have much to do with her people (who were of the established Church and therefore suspicious of dissenters), but he dreaded any estrangement. Kate was their only supporter.

The Sligo community was another hurdle to be crossed. Bessie St Leger, staunchly Establishment, was highly put out about the engagement, though Noble was relieved that her husband, Noblett, greeted him as usual in the street. By February all Sligo was talking and the Reverend Shepperd received a letter from 'Miss L.' enquiring what the position was – very kind and sincere, but 'open-mouthed'.

In the event Miss Lawson chose to leave his church. Tongues no doubt continued to wag, but a month later, he announced his forthcoming marriage formally to members of his congregation, who, on the whole, took it well.

Janey was to be of great comfort to her ageing husband for 10 blissfully happy years. With him she would adopt two of Kate's children. When his sight failed she read to Noble in the evenings. She herself lived on, much loved by her foster children, until in 1892 she died during an epidemic of influenza.

12

In Carrick Town

Carrick-on-Shannon 1860-73

Even in marriage, Kate Mitchell's addiction to her own family remained the most powerful force in her life. She was constantly going back to Sligo. She was in Sligo in August 1860 when Michael wrote to her hoping she was no longer suffering from 'morning illness'. Her mother Bidz Cullen was in her last frailty and Kate stayed with her in the house on the Mall, where Jemmy kept a splendid garden. Michael joked with her, calling her his 'truant wife'; and urging her to buy any silks she desired from Sally Faussett, the calf would pay for it. The following year she stayed at the Ulster Bank, where Michael's brother James was now manager.

Their first son, George (after Michael's father) Cullen (after Kate's family), was born in the spring of 1861, and Kate's mother, Bidz, paid a visit to Carrick to see him. On her return to Sligo, Jemmy was there to meet Bidz, Janey had baked a hot cake, and Bessie came over as Noblett was away. Bidz was waking in the mornings with pain in her head, yet she could still regale Kate with snippets of gossip.

> The people of Sligo are mad on the Turkish bath, there is nothing else talked of, some for it and others against it. Mrs Gordon has been taking them for rheumatism. What we heard about her with regard to her going to increase the population has no foundation. Perhaps the bath may have some effect.

And she marvelled at the bereaved Mary Palmer, 'going about in a scoop shaped bonnet without a veil or Widow's cap. . . . She wears a small white linen Collar instead of a crape one.'

Bidz Cullen, 'the little lady from Clare', died later that year. Jemmy and Janey left Sligo, and came to Carrick-on-Shannon, Jemmy to stay in lodgings, and Janey to live at the bank house, where she was invaluable to Kate as the family increased. Janey loved them all as if they were her own children. John James, named after Kate and Janey's father, and Bidz Finucane, after their mother, were born in 1862 and 1863. Eventually, with Gilly, Sue, Jinny and Baby (Victoria Diana), Michael and Kate would have seven children.[1]

---

1. It was common during the 19th century to give the children family names, beginning with

'I never prayed for them that they should be rich or handsome', Kate wrote in her *Memoir*, 'but I did pray that they might not be 'thick'; and that they should have a sense of humour. This prayer I believe was granted, for there was not one of them who did not know how to laugh.'

Brother Jemmy continued to drift. For a few years after the Famine, he had had a temporary post in the Poor Law Office. Then, when regiments were called out for the Crimean War, he had been put in command of a company in the Leitrim Militia. When the regiments later disbanded, he was without employment again until 1871, when he got the Quartermastership of the Regiment. But he was happiest philandering, and advising his sisters about their gardens.

Kate wrote in his defence that he was a very well read man, with refined tastes, fond of poetry and reading, simply spoilt by his mother, who never let him want for anything, and allowed him to fall into lazy indolent habits. He eventually married Sydney Kirkwood, who was the second daughter of Thomas Kirkwood of Clongoonagh, and sister of Kate's great friend Anna Kirkwood, and of Diana's former admirer, Andrew. They lived first in a cottage on Liberty Hill, and then rented Shannon Lodge from Diana l'Herrault – after whom they named their first daughter.

In October 1862, Kate went to stay with her sister Bessie in Sligo, bringing George and baby 'Jack' – later he was always called Johnny – to be photographed. Michael enquired how the 'gorsoons'[2] were liked by her relatives. He became impatient as she continued to stay away. He was busy, apart from banking. He had cut the oats, and was ready to 'attack the praties', the heifer and calf were likely to sell well, and he hoped to bring Bob the horse down to Sligo and sell him there. The Cricket Dinner had gone off pleasantly. But, busy or not, he was lonely, and tired of housekeeping.

Noble Shepperd found the same thing after his marriage with Janey. The Cullen clannishness was a strain on the most selfless relationships. Janey, or 'The Sheperdess' as Michael now called her, was in Carrick in 1865, awaiting the birth of Kate's third son, Michael Thomas (his father's names; 'Gilly' to the family). Noble wrote to her,

> Yesterday we were two months married. – Tomorrow we shall be nine weeks, and you will be one third of that time away from me. Well, it is, as we have before said, in the performance of duty, but it is curious, – I certainly sometimes feel as if I were not married at all.

---

the father's father, and alternating between the two families thereafter. None of the daughters were called after Kate or Bessie. Sue was named after Michael's mother Susan Langstaff, Jinny (Jane Georgina) after the sisters closest to Kate, Victoria Diana after Diana de l'Herrault and probably her second husband, though Victoria, being the monarch's name, was fashionable at the time.

2.   'Garsún' is the Irish for a boy.

Extracts from a book, measuring 3 x 2.5 cms., made by Johnny Mitchell for his sisters Jenny and Victoria Diana Mitchell, c.1875. Private collection, Dublin.

Despite these irritations, relations remained amiable between the sisters and their husbands. 1864, when their family still numbered only three, was the last time that Kate stayed away from home for any considerable time. With the Sheperdess, she took herself for the summer to Rosses Point, the

The Metal Man, Rosses Point, Sligo, c.1912, by Jack B. Yeats (1871-1957).
(Photograph courtesy of the National Gallery of Ireland, no. 3831.)

little village to the north of Sligo town, which could be pooled with sun or mist some days, or torn by wild Atlantic winds even in summer. She and Janey had known the beckoning islands of the bay, the swift flow of the tide up the channel, and the springy walk to the Far Point, since their own childhood. They must have felt at home with the people of the Point, beneath the airy sky. Kitzy had a nurse for the children, 'fat nurse', and Michael allowed her the indulgence of an inside car, 'as you and fat nurse cannot care children on an outsider.' But he warned her not to be coerced into overpayment.

Decorating while Kate was away, Michael dined at Hatley Manor. The next generation would accuse Michael of over-extravagance. It was related to his generosity of heart; and he looked after Kate well, sending butter and eggs to her at Rosses Point, chicken, pears and lobsters; and – when she was away in the autumn – he made sure of getting some game to her – a brace of grouse, a hare, a wild duck. He remembered the household necessities as well, and travelling down by train to Sligo, he brought with him tea and candles. August 18, 1864, was his birthday, and he wrote to Kitzy in one of his sober moods,

> 41 years ago I came into this World of Change and trouble, with some gleams of Sunshine here and there, and I was Struck by the text in my little Book this morning: 'Surely goodness and mercy shall follow thee all the days of thy life'.

While Kate was at Rosses Point, her sisters and their husbands were holidaying at Mullaghmore in Sligo. Almost as soon as they arrived, the nervy Victor was writing to Michael, apprehensive about the health of his patron, Charles St George – St George was in Italy.

> Diana Dreamt of a letter & saw a large one at the candle, I was so sure to get bad news that I went undressed to get the letter at the Postman.

Victor's nervous intuition was prophetic. Charles Manners St George, landlord of Carrick, did die, on November 22, aged 78. He came home to be buried in the grounds of his seat, Hatley Manor, in a mausoleum with his arms carved over the door.[3]

Because of her marriage to Michael, Kate had now to conform to the Church of Ireland. Kate anyway – despite her instinctive loyalty to the Rev-

---

3. Ineri Christina St George, his wife, kept on Hatley Manor in Carrick, and died at La Spezia about 20 years later. Their heir – they had no children – was a niece, Petronella Alberg. Charles St George had a large collection of paintings in his house in Fitzwilliam Place in Dublin, and one of these, a Madonna and Infant Christ, Kate remembered, hung over the communion table in Carrick church.

erend Shepperd and the Sligo conventicle – was fond of the Rector of Carrick, the Reverend William Percy, and his family whom she had known from childhood. When a girl, she recalled in her memoir, she had been invited to stay at their place, Drumliffin, about four or five miles from Carrick.

> They brought us out in their wagonette which they had had for some years, these machines having come into fashion then. . . . The old Rector was very humorous. He used to call me 'Catty, Honey, Dear.' We slept in his study, the house being full at the time, and he said to me 'if you are sleepless in the night, just get up and play a tune on the Cello.' He himself used often to get up at 4 o'c. in the morning to practise this instrument. The girls sang very well, but their father used to tell them after this that they need not think they could sing my songs.

Kate always prided herself on her good voice, but she did acknowledge the Percy girls, later Mrs Johnson and Mrs French – the latter married to Christopher French of Cloonaquin, and mother of the immortal Percy French – as beauties of their day.

She still cared about clothes, and recalls in her *Memoir* that the crinoline was very fashionable in Carrick-on-Shannon. 'I may mention here', she interpolates in an account of some people in Sligo,

> that I never wore the crinoline, being disgusted with the extravagance of the pitch to which it was worn in Carrick, the wearers often finding on entering their seats in Church that it had ascended to their ears, where it remained till some friendly hand pulled it down. Until it assumed a normal appearance I never wore it, which pleased my husband, although I believe Mr Mooney, the Curate of Carrick, said, 'if Mrs Mitchell knew her own interest, she would wear the crinoline.' This remark, when retailed to me, made no alteration in my views on the matter.

> It was a great relief to the eye to turn from the extravagance of the crinoline to the simple fashion of the Galway Cloak (the Claddagh Cloak) which was also worn at this time in various colours. I had one a lovely shade of blue, given to me by my sister Bessie, and I found it very comfortable when on my wedding trip. It was much stared at in Scotland, not having been introduced there at that time.

The Cullen passion for gardens, born in her at Skreeney, never abated. An old couple, a Mr and Mrs Wynne, who lived in a cottage on Liberty Hill had a little greenhouse, which they showed to visitors with pride.

> The humorous people of Carrick named them 'Adam and Eve'. . . . They generally contrived to get the newest flowers, and with them I remember first seeing a 'pelargonium', which was then accounted a

great novelty. It was called 'Lowndes Perfection': it was a beautiful pink with black back leaves. At this time, the only flower approaching the Pelargonium was the oak-leaf geranium with the small pink flower. The 'Fair Helen', the white pelargonium – also came in now.

As in her childhood, she took a great interest in the beggars and oddities of the neighbourhood. Maggie Tighe was a Protestant, an elderly woman, who sat at the end of the church. Church money was dealt out to her, and other mendicants, each Sunday after service. Every winter the parish gave her a stuff dress, usually made of wincey,[4] with a new plaid shawl; and each summer she received a cotton dress. These all had a bath in the wash-tub soon after she received them, for her mania was washing.

> One day, she went to get her accustomed dole from Madame de l'Herrault at Shannon Lodge. She [Diana] called out of the window to her, and said she would not give her anything as she had heard that Maggie had abused 'Mr Victor' behind her back.
>
> Oh! is it me to abuse Misther Victor?' said Maggie, 'Sure I wouldn't do the like.'
>
> Well, you did,' said Madame, 'and you won't get anything.' Maggie, seeing the case was hopeless turned to go, and then, half turning back, called out in a loud voice, 'And a sore chuck he is, Victor!' And immediately made good her retreat.

Another character Kate describes is Paddy Lavin, a dwarf, who wore flat cap, trousers of corduroy and a grey frieze body coat given him by the town – typical garments of the period to judge by contemporary paintings. 'He had the reputation of being very honest, and, though very small and odd-looking, was not a wicked dwarf, but had a pleasant expression and his face was all smiles when he received a gift from an old friend.'

Michael was closely involved in Kiltoghert Parish during the years leading up to Disestablishment in 1870, when he was elected to the new Church of Ireland vestry (no more would he talk about his 'own dear Church of England'!) He continued to be a prominent Mason, as was his brother Adam in Birr. His years as Prince Mason and Master of Lodge 854 were renowned long after his death as the great years of the Carrick Lodge.[5] In May 1872, he received a further honour when he was designated Knight of the Sun (Chevalier du Soleil) of the 28th Degree.

He was a good father to his increasing family. He encouraged sensible

---

4.   A strong warm cloth, with a linen warp and a woollen weft.
5.   A. O'Connor, *Concord Lodge, 854, Carrick-on-Shannon, 1797-1897*, Concord Lodge, 1897. p. 16.

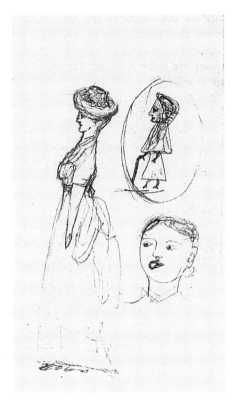

Childhood drawing c.1880 by
Victoria Diana Mitchell.
Private collection, Dublin.

enjoyable reading, brought them to church, and dined with them in the parlour at 4. When their eldest son was ten, he arranged that he should attend Elphin Diocesan School, an establishment of 100 years standing; and from that time George made his home in Sligo with Aunt and Uncle Shepperd.

Michael had a special rapport with his second daughter, Susan, red headed like her mother, pretty and intelligent, and plans were made to send her to the Masonic School in Dublin.

Generous to others, Michael was also generous to himself and he enjoyed the good things of life, but his attempts at discipline, involving a 'claret régime', came too late. Kidney disease took its toll, and he was forced to resign from his position as manager of the Bank of Ireland. Just a month later, in October 1873, Kate's Archangel finally rested his pinions.

He was buried with full Masonic honours in Kiltoghert churchyard. The memorial raised by his fellow masons may still be seen in the sanctuary of the church, a handsome plaque beside the organ.

Kate's reference to her husband's death in the memoir is made in passing, totally without emotion, and with no indication of the heartbreak she must have suffered through an upheaval that must have hit her even more hardly than the crucial exodus from Skreeney. She had to leave Carrick-on-Shannon, barely 40 years of age, to start life anew with her family of seven and the meagre pension the bank had to offer.

Her lot was not singular. There were many young widows of the period in similar circumstances, dependent on their husbands, having to adapt to radical changes in their style of living on bereavement. Kate had the advantage that she was resourceful, and she could rely for support on the sisters and the family to whom she was so close. Her disposition prevented her from being cowed by such a major blow, and her innate sense of humour obviously came to her rescue.

Following her fortunes through the pages of her memoir, too, it is plain why she scribbled in under the initial title *Reminiscences of My Life* a more specific sub-title, *My Candid Opinion of My Relatives*. The Cullen family had been and would always be her consuming interest.

She visited Carrick-on-Shannon in later years, noting in her memoir,

> Carrick is very much the same now as it was in those days, I believe, but many of the old people have passed away and many new, of whom I know but little, are there and we have little communication with it, but I still have a strong regard for the old place, where I spent many happy days. David Browne, who was accountant and teller in the Provincial Bank . . . succeeded my husband as manager.

Conclusion

'I left Carrick on the death of my dear husband,' Kate wrote in her matter-of-fact way in the concluding pages of her memoir, 'and went to live in Sligo, in order to place the boys in Schools suited to their years.

> The eldest was already at the Diocesan School (as I mentioned before). He was living with his Aunt and his Uncle the Rev. Noble Sheppard, as was also my eldest daughter Bidz. Mr Sheppard died in 1874 and Mrs Sheppard left the Manse and went to live on the Mall taking George and Bidz with her.

> When I came to Sligo I stayed first at William Ingham's (former lodgings of my Husband, where he stayed before he was married) in George's Street. Finding that these lodgings were not very agreeable, I left and took a house on the Mall belonging to Mr Wynne (Mr Olpherts being the agent). I had with me my four children – Johnny, Gilly, Jenny and Victoria – Susan, whom I had intended to send to the Masonic School, having been taken by her Aunts, who lived in Dublin. I had also with me my old nurse Mary Cleary [a Sligo woman], and a maid, Katie Collins, whom I had brought from Carrick.

So ends her account of life in Carrick-on-Shannon, in Sligo and the West in the middle of the last century. Moving to Sligo, she resorted to taking in lodgers in order to make ends meet. Out of their seven children, George and Bidz were adopted by Aunt and Uncle Shepperd who were already their guardians, and Susan by Aunt Wegg in Dublin. There is no reference to Susan (later the satirist and mystic poet of the Irish Renaissance), in the engagement diaries that survive, other than mentions of two letters from her, and, on May 14, 1884, she heard that Susan had 'passed Trinity 1st Class Certificate'. Later their lives would be closely interlinked.

The younger children went to the Misses Blyth's Infant School in Stephen Street, where Jack Yeats, then living with his Pollexfen grandparents, was in the same class as Victoria Diana. Bidz taught at the school as soon as she had qualified. Gifted as a singer like her mother, she married a bank clerk at a comparatively young age. Victoria and Susan would later teach at the same – now renowned – school.

Bidz Brabazon, Kate's eldest daughter, and her family, with a maid, 1895.
Private collection, Dublin.

Johnny and Gilly (young Michael) were to follow George into their father's profession (described by George as 'the living tomb', the 'charnel house'; 'by the time you are in it you will have forgotten how the devil you got in at all, and only wonder how the devil you are to get out,' he warned Gilly), one in the Provincial Bank, the other in the Bank of Ireland.

Content that the elder boys were settled in steady positions, Kate, after the years of struggle, found a post agreeable to herself. The County Club, of two years' standing, was looking for a stewardess, and, with her background and hospitable personality, she was the perfect candidate.

In May 1881, she auctioned the furniture she would not be taking with her from the house in the Mall – the drinking glasses and chairs, the chiffoniers and the Loo table, with its memories of carefree card parties at Skreeney – and moved with her widowed sister Janey, the remaining children and their faithful old Nurse to live in Wine Street.

Christmas in the 1880s, from a drawing by Beatrice Glenavy (1883-1971), illus-
trating Cuala Card (68), 'The Red Berried Holly'.

The County Club, opposite the Wesley Chapel, which Kate, now revert-
ing to her low church leanings, attended as an alternative to the Congregational
Church in Stephen Street, was a fine stone building, its three storeys standing
back a little from the street, the entrance a wide elegant doorway. Its rival,
the Constitutional Club in Stephen Street, was founded in December of that
year, and soon had a membership of about 160, attracting mainly politicians
and intellectuals.[1] The two clubs sometimes came together. But Kate was in
her element in the County, where the well born and the military met to dine
or to spend a night in town. Visiting judges used the Club during the
Assizes.

The continual round of activity suited her energetic disposition. She

---

1.   W. G. Wood-Martin, *History of Sligo*, vol. 7, Dublin 1892, p. 182.

continued for five years providing accomodation and sustenance on a small scale, day in, day out: relieving her duties with an occasional afternoon at Rosses Point, or with Diana de l'Herrault or Jemmy and Dido visiting from Carrick, or an hour snatched in the Mall with Bessie St Leger.

In 1886 she gave up her post as stewardess. She was suffering increasingly from headaches, and probably found the pace of the Club was too much for her. On June 12, there was a riot in Sligo, with windows smashed and great consternation. The following day, Whit Sunday, the troops arrived. After this, there are no personal records since her engagement diaries come to an end.

She was now in her mid-50s, and her own large family of brothers and sisters, of whom she was the youngest, began to reduce. She would outlive them all. In 1887, Bessie St Leger died. She had been a widow since 1872, and an invalid for years, but retained her vivacity and spirit till the last, Kate spending many an afternoon by her bedside in the grand house on the Mall.

Francis Nesbitt Cullen, the brother next to Kate whom she still remembered as the merry playmate of their youth, was next to go, on October 2, 1889.[2] Francis, according to his sister, had gone from the Poor Law Office to a cadetship in the Royal Irish Constabulary. From Dublin his career took him to Lowtherstown, afterwards to French Park and then to Tuam. He married one of their Clare cousins, the eldest daughter of Andrew Finucane of Ennistymon House, who had a large fortune.

Francis was in Galway during the Fenian disturbances in the late 60s. Subsequently he applied for a 'quiet' station at Tullamore, in King's County. In the early 1880s, he was sent to Belfast as Town Inspector, and, Kate related in her *Memoir,*

> then had the luck to come in for the Belfast Riots in 1887. After this he was made a Divisional Commissioner and Assistant Inspector General of the RIC; he was again overworked – attending Land League Meetings and trying to keep the Peace between Land Leaguers and Orange men. He was then stationed at Armagh, and having attended a Political Demonstration at Dungannon he came home very ill, and after about three weeks illness succumbed . . . in the sixtieth year of his age.

> He was a very fine looking man, a noble presence, a good and clever officer, greatly beloved by his men, a strictly honorable and perfect gentleman, temperate in his habits, and a most kind husband; he is buried in the Churchyard of Manorhamilton, within sight of the old home where he and I played as children. . . .

---

2.   According to his gravestone in Manorhamilton Churchyard. In her *Memoir*, Kate records the date as July 1890.

Kate's financial situation eased considerably after the death of her sister, Diana de l'Herrault, in 1890 (though Diana left Shannon Lodge to Jemmy), and after Janey Shepperd fell a victim to the fatal 'flu of 1892. In 1896, John Marcus, her remaining brother, died in New Jersey. Kate's final link with Skreeney, except for Georgina who lived into the new century, was now broken.

After leaving the County Club, Kate had lived in John Street. She moved to a more comfortable but plain house with a single fanlight in the Mall, where circumstances became more to her liking – she kept a pony and trap and a man, as well as two indoor servants. It was a leisurely cultured life. Her daughters were singers like herself, much in demand at concerts; and Victoria Diana, who married a musician in 1899, would be the backbone of the Sligo Féis until her death 60 years later.

It was in 1899, when her daughter Susan came to live with her in Sligo, that Kate embarked upon her extensive *Memoir*, dictating to Susan as she reminisced. Susan, who had lived with aunts until they died at advanced years, had come anew to her own family, and was fascinated by Kate's constant reminiscing about the Cullens.

Susan's interest in the family must have been whetted too by the recent reading of her horoscope by George Pollexfen (uncle of the Yeatses). Pollexfen had told Susan that the sun was a dominant planet at her birth, and so a constant influence on her. 'The 10th house the Midheaven is generally taken as the mothers House,' he informed her, 'and you will see Leo of the Suns

Victoria Diana Franklin, Kate's youngest daughter, c.1920.
Private collection, Dublin.

Harry Franklin, husband of Victoria Diana Mitchell. Private collection, Dublin.

sign upon that house so that I should opine that you take your sun disposition and characteristics from your mother.'

After Susan moved to Dublin to join Horace Plunkett as sub-editor of his new publication the *Irish Homestead*, Kate had the opportunity of meeting the writers and performers of the Irish Literary Renaissance. George Russell and the Abbey Theatre company holidaying at Rosses Point would visit her and enjoy her hospitality in the house on the Mall. Despite the increasing weight that came with old age, and the rheumatism for which she sought relief in Lisdoonvarnagh, drinking the waters, she still enjoyed life and saw its humorous side.

In 1908, after the tragic death of Gilly who was epileptic, Kate moved to Dublin to live with Susan and Jinny. Despite her low church inclinations and

Susan L. Mitchell, Kate's second daughter, drawn by herself on a postcard sent to her brother Johnny Mitchell, December 22, 1905.
(Courtesy of Trinity College Library, Manuscripts Room.)

her conservative view of politics, from both of which her daughters diverged, Kate with her generous personality fitted well into the household in Frankfort Avenue off the Rathgar Road. Her sense of humour prevailed at all times, as did her love of life.

Susan was a close friend of Lily Yeats, and, like Constance Markiewicz who lived not far away, they were proud of their ties with the West. Kate presided with ease at Susan's literary evenings, and it was at about this time that Susan persuaded her to augment the memoir with greater detail about the personalities and fortunes of her numerous family. The passing of her old

*16 Frankfort Avenue,
Rathgar, Dublin.*
(Author's photograph.)

family servant and friend, Mary Cleary, who accompanied Kate to Dublin, may have sparked off this second series of reminiscences.

Catherine Theresa Cullen died in April 1913 at her daughter's home in Dublin, still alert, if her memory was not what it had been. Appreciations came in from many quarters, for besides her warmth and her valued gift for crossing social barriers within and beyond the bounds of Protestantism, her changing fortunes had brought her into contact with a diversity of people.

The poet Seumas O'Sullivan, writing to Susan, remembered her as 'the handsome old lady who gave regal hospitality in the Mall'. However the tribute Kate would probably have treasured most was a letter from an old servant, Thomas Farrell, who now had his own private hotel in Carrick-on-Shannon. Writing to commiserate, he lamented Kate's passing, 'the last of a good old Co. [County] family – & fancy what we are meeting nowadays.'

Sources of the Chapter Titles

All of the titles are taken from poems by Susan L. Mitchell, published in *The Living Chalice* (1913) and *Odes to the Immortality of Certain Persons in Ireland* (1913).

Chapter 1   *The Yule Log*

Chapter 2   *The Yule Log*

Chapter 3   *The Tryst*

Chapter 4   *George Moore Comes to Ireland*

Chapter 5   *The Mistletoe*

Chapter 6   *A Dream*

Chapter 7   *The Heart's Low Door*

Chapter 8   *Love in Heaven*

Chapter 9   *Love in Heaven*

Chapter 10   *Exile*

Chapter 11   *The Kiss*

Chapter 12   *Carrick*

Appendix

Four poems by Susan L. Mitchell

Carrick

I will not walk these roads of pain,
I will turn back to youth again.
'Tis full sunlight, though past the noon,
The night will not come very soon,
And if you haste we may lie down
Before sunset in Carrick town.

O brothers, sisters, come with me.
The old house still stands there, you see,
My little red-haired Tories, come,
For none can shut the door of home.
We're safe before the sun goes down,
And sleep is sweet in Carrick town.

O hide me, Carrick, shut me in.
Here in your little streets begin
Again for me the young surprise
Of life, give back the eager eyes,
The bounding hearts, the hands that clung,
The songs our comrade voices sung.

See our own window set so high
To catch the wonder of the sky.
Come Brown Eyes, Blue Eyes, Curly Head.
O come, my living, come, my dead.
O Death, how did you find the way
You tread so certainly to-day?

No bigger than a bulrush, I
Beside the rushy Shannon cry.

There are no children on the shore,
The singing voices sing no more,
The sea draws all her rivers down,
And love has sailed from Carrick town.

[From *The Living Chalice* (new ed.),
Dublin, Maunsel, 1913]

Ode to the British Empire

God of the Irish Protestant,
   Lord of our proud Ascendancy,
Soon there'll be none of us extant,
    We want a few plain words with thee.
       Thou know'st our hearts are always set
       On what we get, on what we get.

The landlords with the bonus fly,
   The gold upon the plate has ceased;
Without our aristocracy
    We sink below the parish priest.
       Unless their hire thy labourers get
       The Pope may rule in Ireland yet.

You sent us to this Popish land;
   Cromwell and William well did smite,
Delivering into our hand
    The Hittite and the Jebusite.
       The Papishes we burned, and yet
       We don't regret, we don't regret.

We did your dirty work for you,
   And incidentally likewise
To us some profit did accrue
    (You'll understand and sympathise).
       Now one by one of each asset
       You've robbed us, this we can't forget.

The tithes and the Establishment
   You took, but still to you we clung:
Off went each fat emolument,
    We smiled although our hearts were wrung.
       Beneath that smile our teeth were set,
       The worrum wouldn't turrn yet.

Though we were growing moribund,
　　With all your acts we still agreed;
We had the Sustentation Fund,
　　You had the Athanasian Creed.
　　　　The Commination Service yet
　　　　Is ours – and do not you forget!

We shouted long, 'God save the King!'
　　And damned the Papacy to hell.
'Twere easy to reverse the thing
　　And send you English all to . . . well
　　　　We needn't mention names, but yet
　　　　We'd see you there without regret.

God of the Irish Protestant,
　　You have grown hideous in our sight;
You're not the kind of god we want.
　　Rise, Sons of William, rise and smite!
　　　　New gods we'll serve, and with them yet
　　　　We'll get all there is left to get!

[From *Aids to the Immortality of Certain Persons in Ireland,
Charitably Administered* (new ed.), Dublin, Maunsel, 1913]

Anti-Recruiting Song

He took the English shilling, his Bible oath he swore,
To serve the King of England. He left the Shannon shore.
He learned to square his shoulders and tune his Irish ear,
To speak the sort of language no decent boy should hear.

It was for great adventures he left old Carrick town,
Where life was dull and narrow and he had no renown.
An appetite for fighting he'd got in many a row,
And he could wield a blackthorn as Leitrim boys know how.

He went out in the trooper and surely he was found,
Where bullets rained the thickest he bravely stood his ground;
He kept the English soldiers from panic in the fray,
For there's not a boy in Leitrim knows how to run away.

He didn't see much glory, and he didn't get much good,
In most unrighteous causes he bravely shed his blood;

The best years of his manhood he spent across the foam,
And when they'd no more use for him they took and sent him home.

He'd bullets in his right arm, he'd bullets in his leg,
He had no *grá* [love] for working and he had no leave to beg;
The peelers had an eye on him, twice he's been in quod,
Now he's in Carrick Workhouse – Glory be to God!

[From *Aids to the Immortality of Certain Persons in Ireland,
Charitably Administered* (new ed.), Dublin, Maunsel, 1913]

The Greenlands

I went up the Greenlands at the Rosses long ago,
Running, stumbling, just a child, small and very wise.
It was well I came from heaven to see the blue bells grow,
And the bright sun's happy thoughts unfold before my eyes.

I was new to human spech, few human words had I,
But immortal language was written all around.
Well I knew the message of the earth and sky
And the short sweet flowers that grew upon the sandy ground.

I held within my little hands the keys of life and death.
From every leaf and blade of grass an old sweet wisdom came,
And in my heart strange flowers sprang up with every hurrying breath,
I saw Ben Bulben as a god, amethyst and flame.

I never saw the Greenlands for many a heavy year,
For I grew old and foolish with the wisdom of the town.
The lofty ways of dreaming for me were full of fear.
I loved my cage and was content with pacing up and down.

My soul stole to the Greenlands all in a dream one night,
I saw them stretching wide and fair up to the gates of gold.
I saw my thoughts in quiet flocks move upwards to the light,
And I, their shepherd, went with them to an eternal fold.

When Death, my gentle nurse, shall call and bid me hasten back
On the high path the bright ones trod my feet might go astray,
But down by Sligo there's a road lies near the homeward track,
And from the Greenlands into heaven is but a little way.

[From *The Living Chalice* (new ed.), Dublin, Maunsel, 1913]

Index of Persons

[Page references for illustrations are in italics]

Index of Places